SEA ROBINS, TRIGGERFISH & OTHER OVERLOOKED SEAFOOD

SEA ROBINS, TRIGGERFISH & OTHER OVERLOOKED SEAFOOD

The Complete Guide to Preparing and Serving Bycatch

CHEF MATTHEW PIETSCH AND JAMES O. FRAIOLI

FOREWORD BY FABIEN COUSTEAU

PHOTOGRAPHY BY
MATTHEW PIETSCH
DONALD LESKO
JAIMIE SKRIBA
SANDRA GUNNETT

Skyhorse Publishing

Skyhorse Publishing books may be purchased in bulk at special discounts for sales promotion, corporate gifts, fund-raising, or educational purposes. Special editions can also be created to specifications. For details, contact the Special Sales Department, Skyhorse Publishing, 307 West 36th Street, 11th Floor, New York, NY 10018 or info@skyhorsepublishing.com.

Skyhorse® and Skyhorse Publishing® are registered trademarks of Skyhorse Publishing, Inc.®, a Delaware corporation.

Visit our website at www.skyhorsepublishing.com.

10 9 8 7 6 5 4 3 2 1

Library of Congress Cataloging-in-Publication Data is available on file.

Cover design by Jenny Zamenak
Interior design by Jenny Zamenak
Cover photo provided by Matthew Pietsch

Print ISBN: 978-1-5107-2642-0
Ebook ISBN: 978-1-5107-2643-7

Printed in China

This book is dedicated to the efforts and individuals who work diligently to protect and preserve our ocean and its diverse ecosystems

CONTENTS

ACKNOWLEDGMENTS

The authors would like to personally thank:

Brooke Peterson, Paul Zemitzsch, Fabien Cousteau, Nicole Frail and the team at Skyhorse Publishing, and Sharlene Martin of Martin Literary Management.

Chef Matthew Pietsch would like to personally acknowledge:

Sara Bakale: Without your input, friendship, contribution, and support, "Our life aquatic" wouldn't exist.

Rob Nicol, Mark Schrock, Steve Darpel, and Casey Longton: Business partners and friends who have provided the support necessary for this publication to exist.

Matthew Campbell: For his thoughtful and knowledgeable wine pairings presented alongside the recipes.

Parents John & Ingrid Pietsch: For always supporting me, my wacky ideas, and providing unconditional love and guidance.

David Geen: For sponsoring me every step of the way, providing constant support and guidance, and for always listening. Gratitude and love to the entire staff at the Douglas Marriott.

The management, staff, friends, family, and guests of Salt of the Earth and Principle Food & Drink.

Donald Lesko: For the incredible guidance and support for much of the photography in this book, Jamie Skriba and Sandi Gunnett for intensively curated collaborative photography and capturing the essence of Salt of the Earth.

Mike Kenat, Gerald, Gary, Jerry, and Gibby, R&B for all the things and stuff, Austin's Moustache, Paul Parrish, Dan the Man, Schmiggles, Jaguar, Two Fists Nelson, El Presidente, Emily Anstadt, Tucker's Moustache, Miles Davis, KL, Mr. Hahnsworth, Bob "the flopper," Norm—he's my brother but we're not related, Brad Baller, Fornesto, Cheffry Bailey, Andrew Briggs, Tony with the awesome hair, Rebecca Duboise Idaho, Paolo Franzese, Gary Poirier, Fred Bourney, Beth Robinson, Anne call me back, Matt Millar, Sue from the hardware store, Fennville, Michigan, and Sweetwater Donuts.

To every single one of our hardworking, dedicated growers and producers, past and present; you are the intention of our work and we celebrate your commitment to our local food system, your stewardship to the earth, supporting our business, and for assisting us to serve our guests.

INCIDENTAL CATCH

Incidental catch (noun) \in(t)-se-'dent-l\'kach\

Those fish caught merely by chance or without intention or calculation and retained.

Example: Hooking and keeping a grouper when fishing for snapper.

BYCATCH

Bycatch (noun) \'bi-,'kach\

The portion of a commercial fishing catch that consists of fish and other marine species caught unintentionally. These species may be incidental or discarded back to the sea.

Example: Catching flounder and sea robins in a bottom trawl intended for cod and keeping the cod and flounder and discarding the sea robins.

FOREWORD

by
Fabien Cousteau

For three generations, my family has expressed one of the most fundamental truths of our planet . . .

"There is no waste in Nature."

When we humans leave Nature alone, it mostly takes care of itself. All creatures and plants have a role in life. The food chain works efficiently. There is a life cycle for all things that are born or sprout: grow, eventually die, decompose, and the cycle begins again.

It is no different in the ocean. From zooplankton to orcas, seaweed to coral reefs, and sharks to rays, it's a "city under the sea," as my good friend, Dr. Richard Murphy, likes to explain. Every living thing has a role in keeping the ocean healthy.

Humans, however, are an inherently wasteful species. From common trash in landfills to plastic in our ocean to nutritious food simply discarded, we throw away a staggering volume of items and food products. Most people are becoming aware of the calamity due to overfishing. We are depleting our once bountiful ocean—with some fish species disappearing by 90 percent or more.

This is not to say fishing is a bad practice and consumers should stop eating fish; the role of the fisherman goes back thousands of years and has provided a living for families for generations. Our family has always supported fishermen, but we caution that overfishing certain species and using industrialized techniques that strip the ocean clean are not in the best interest of fishermen themselves.

Once a species collapses due to overfishing, it is gone and likely gone forever. Fishing with methods that keep our ocean's bounty stable means many more generations of fishermen can continue their profession for future lifetimes.

How a fish eventually gets to your table is a story of many possible chapters.

Commercial fishing on a larger scale targets high-profit fish to meet the needs of restaurants, grocery stores, and individual consumers, but what often occurs is a side product known as bycatch, which are species caught accidentally and generally not profitable for fishermen despite many of these fish being perfectly edible. These fish are plucked from fishing nets and simply thrown overboard dead or barely alive.

If bycatch cannot be properly returned to the sea, then what is the best course of action to take? That's what this book, *Sea Robins, Triggerfish & Overlooked Seafood*, is all about.

Fishermen should make a concerted effort to bring their edible bycatch back to the dock and introduce the fish to seafood distributers. They should educate and encourage the distributors

to promote and sell these unfamiliar species to the restaurants, which, in turn, can promote and sell them to their customers. This new seafood movement will help eliminate waste while creating awareness and building a demand for delicious and ocean-friendly seafood.

Introducing underutilized fish also takes pressure off the heavily targeted species like the rapidly depleted tuna and swordfish and other species, while concentrating on those lesser-known species, which, again, are perfectly edible and taste good.

Is consuming bycatch the real solution to protecting heavily targeted species while replenishing our oceans? Maybe, but it's also the start to a much larger puzzle. Through properly educating ourselves and future generations, we can begin to stop the degradation of our environment and ecosystems.

In an ideal world, fishermen would not be able to throw back certain fish. But, until

then, let's encourage seafood consumers to try those under-appreciated species and share their seafood experiences with friends and dinner guests so they, too, can feel good about supporting sustainable food systems.

I am pleased and honored to support a book like *Sea Robins, Triggerfish & Overlooked Seafood* while educating myself about the many new species now being unloaded on today's docks.

Let's celebrate these other fish in the sea by enjoying a bounty of recipes assembled by Executive Chef Matthew Pietsch and James Beard award-winning author James O. Fraioli as they encourage seafood consumers to support and promote those less common fish while still enjoying quality seafood at an affordable price.

As my father, grandfather, and I always say, everything is connected.

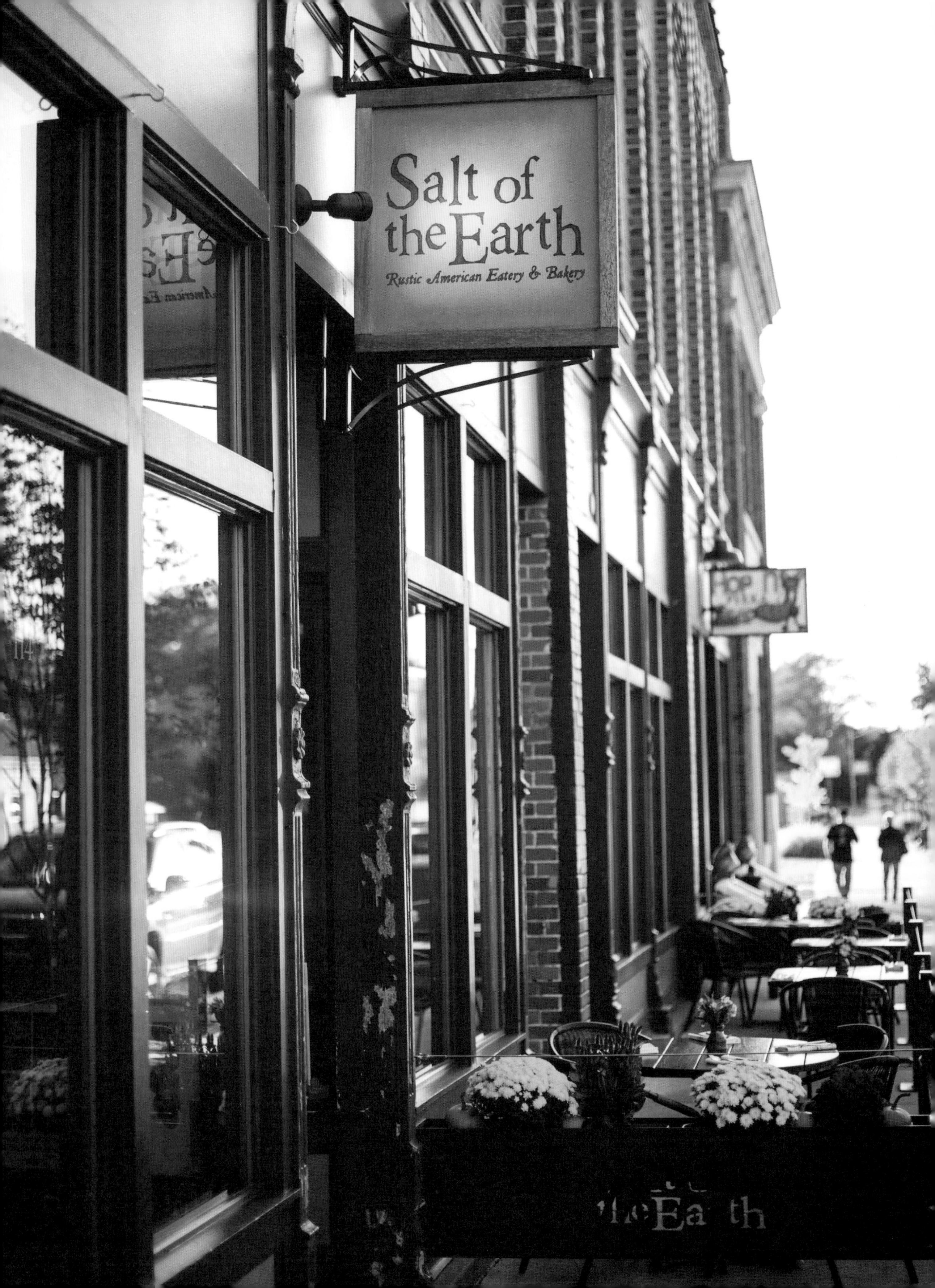
Salt of the Earth
Rustic American Eatery & Bakery

INTRODUCTION

At this very moment, in oceans across the globe, countless boats, small and large, with thousands of miles of nets and lines, are removing millions of fish from the sea. And they're doing so at a rate of billions of pounds every year. Yes, it's the ocean, considered the last truly wild frontier, where we come to behave as commercial hunters in quest of our prey. But, as in most parts of the world, we are too efficient at what we do.

Fish were once viewed as an inexhaustible resource, able to fill nets and put food on our plates without limit for generations to come. We're quickly learning, however, that there just aren't enough fish to go around. The oceans are proving unable to keep up with a growing demand for seafood fueled by population increases and the industrialization of global fishing fleets.

In addition to overfishing, we are also realizing that many marine species that live on the deep-sea floor—seamounts and corals that have grown for thousands of years—are being crushed by commercial fishing vessels, particularly deep-sea trawlers. This fragile underwater wilderness, covering more than 50 percent of our planet and 90 percent of the ocean floor, took millennia to grow, but is being destroyed rapidly by fisheries marauding the sea, scouring everything within their far reach. With modern fishing gear, often undetectable by sight and extremely resilient and efficient at catching the desired fish species—as well as everything else in its path— we are wiping out the ocean.

What is the solution? While fishing industry leaders are realizing the need to reduce such wasteful practices, and with organizations like the World Wildlife Fund working with fisheries to help develop and promote new technologies

and modify gear for more efficient operations, we, as consumers, must also be proactive. We must become accountable for our own behavior and the choices we make as consumers when sitting down at a restaurant or shopping at a supermarket. That is what *Sea Robins, Triggerfish & Overlooked Seafood* is offering out of love for the sea and a concern for its well-being.

Fabien Cousteau's father, Jean-Michel, believes that "If we protect what we love, there is an opportunity to connect to the sea in a very meaningful way, and to spread the word every time we eat or invite people in. It is a connection that begins the slow process of our giving back to what has always been the abundance of the sea."

And he's right—which brings us to the topic of bycatch and why we, as consumers, should consider enjoying and appreciating such fish, whether ordering from a menu or purchasing for home.

According to the US Department of Agriculture, seafood consumption continues to rise, now predicted to increase 7 percent by 2020. One reason for the growing popularity of fish and shellfish during the last decade has been the strong evidence from groups such as the National Academy of Sciences and the Harvard School of Public Health that seafood is among the most

beneficial foods we can eat. All kinds of reasons are suggested, but among the most important of them are the abundant supplies of omega-3 fatty acids in seafood. These have been shown to be essential for childhood development, help reduce the risk of heart disease, strengthen the immune system, and even possibly help prevent such tragic ailments as Alzheimer's disease. These are all certainly reasons to eat as much seafood as we can, not to mention how delicious seafood tastes. Yet, every day across the planet, fishermen continue to discard their bycatch, throwing many species overboard dead or barely alive because the primary concern is collecting only those more profitable fish. Today, bycatch is one of the biggest threats facing marine ecosystems around the world.

According to government estimates, fishermen throw away 2 billion pounds of fish every year.

What these fishermen may not realize—or maybe they do—is that many bycatch species they're pulling up in their nets or at the end of their long-lines are perfectly edible, just as nutritious, and often equally as tasty.

This seafood mindset is very analogous to the American lobster, a prized item enjoyed by many today. Before the nineteenth century, lobster represented poverty. It was a "trash fish" served to servants and lower members of society. The white, succulent meat, which we now savor on special occasions, was fed to prisoners and used as fertilizer and fish bait. So what changed? Did the lobster suddenly evolve into a better-tasting creature? No. Eventually, commercial fishermen decided to bring their lobsters back to the dock, and in the mid-nineteenth century New Yorkers and Bostonians developed a taste for the crustacean. In other words, the different choices made by the fishermen and consumers created buying power to shape market demand. As they brought back more lobster, the demand increased, influencing the supply and bringing even more lobster to the marketplace. Thanks to this one movement, Americans today continue to enjoy lobster across the country.

A similar story can be shared about the monkfish (page 6), considered one of the ugliest fish in the sea and referred to as "poor man's lobster" (after the lobster reached notoriety). But now it is the monkfish—not the lobster—continuing to be caught incidentally in trawls and scallop dredges. And like the American lobster, fishermen are bringing this unusual fish back to the dock, creating a similar demand. Today, monkfish status has increased significantly and is now valued more than cod, haddock, and flounder.

Lobster and monkfish aren't the only delicious options, of course. Many other great-tasting fish in the sea—many fish that are still considered bycatch—are unfortunately discarded as we continue to hunt and deplete the more sought-after species, some to virtual extinction. In the United States alone, fishermen discard approximately 20 percent of what they catch, with some fisheries throwing away more than what they keep. The average shrimp trawler's

haul, for instance, is only 16 percent shrimp. The rest is comprised of fifty or so common species, including edible squid and whelks. In the Gulf of Mexico, in addition to the heavily targeted species, you'll find more than one thousand species of finfish, all of which are edible. And on the west coast of the United States, more than ninety species are caught together in nets and long-lines when fishermen are specifically pursuing groundfish like flounder and halibut.

Like Fabien Cousteau shares in the foreword, what if we didn't discard these perfectly edible species? What if we introduced and prepared these fish for today's seafood aficionados just like they did with the American lobster and monkfish, especially those looking for a change on the menu while simultaneously supporting our fragile planet and reducing man's footprint on Earth? Again, this is what *Sea Robins, Triggerfish & Overlooked Seafood* is about. We're helping to take the pressure off species like swordfish and Bluefin tuna by introducing home cooks to an array of bycatch and incidental

species unloaded on today's docks by fishermen inspired to make a difference. From Whole Roasted Porgy with Sweet Corn, Marinated Pole Beans & Winter Squash (page 112), to Red Rock Crab Cake with Roasted Pepper Mustard and Baby Kale (page 9), to Korean Fried Skate Wings (page 12), it's time America—and the rest of the world—tastes these less popular fish. And that's a good thing. Eating bycatch, like eating offal, is about avoiding waste while creating awareness and building a demand for delicious and ocean-friendly seafood. And by serving bycatch, we are making an important contribution to conservation.

Coauthor Matthew Pietsch, executive chef and owner of Michigan award-winning restaurants Salt of the Earth and Principle Food & Drink, has been driving the West Michigan farm-to-table movement since the day he opened his first restaurant in early 2009. Today, he continues to develop strong relationships with many farmers, producers, and fishermen around the country. His food focus begins with sourcing the highest-quality ingredients and processing these ingredients as simply as possible. Great food cannot be made without such ingredients. We suggest you look for premium-quality ingredients when preparing dishes from the recipes found within. Visit any quality food market, or develop relationships at local farmers' markets and seafood purveyors for your selections. Chef Matthew's restaurants were also created with the intended purpose of offering fresh, sustainable seafood based on traditional preparations and techniques. The recipes found within this cookbook are just that. Whether it is pickle-brined lionfish from the warm Atlantic or pan-seared lingcod from the cold Pacific, the food is as you would expect to find it at Chef Matthew's restaurants.

We would all agree that food is the nourishment of life, but more importantly, it brings families together and enriches the celebration of friends and special events. The kitchen is the centerpiece in every home. It is often the place we find people gathering to share life, laughter, and happiness. It is that familiar feeling, along with building a better understanding of our oceans, that Matthew's restaurants create each day.

Throughout the book are Chef Matthew's favorite recipes, including some unusual spe-

cies for you to improve your skills if you are a little timid about cooking seafood. Of course, no meal is complete without the perfect beverage or glass of fine wine. That's why we've also included pairing suggestions throughout. Finally, sprinkled within the pages are plenty of techniques and tips that can be universally applied to finned fish and shellfish. If Chef Matthew has one caveat in cooking it would be "Cook Simply, Simply Cook!"

Depending on where you live, there's a good chance you won't be able to find every fish in this book at your local market, and that's okay. Many of the seafood items are interchangeable. If you can't find flounder, use sole. Can't find rock crab, use blue crab. Can't find monkfish, use halibut. . . . Keep in mind, however, that we're encouraging you to try those bycatch species that would otherwise be thrown overboard. And with the Internet and airfreight shrinking the globe, ordering fresh seafood direct from distributors and having a box of deliciousness delivered right to your front doorstep is easier than ever. You never know. You might just receive that ice-cold box of sea robins and triggerfish for you to prepare for family and friends. Until then, turn the pages ahead and dive into the exciting culinary experience that awaits!

COMMERCIAL HARVESTING METHODS RESPONSIBLE FOR BYCATCH

Fishermen use many kinds of gear and processes to catch the fish we eat. Here are some of the major methods used in commercial fishing, in which bycatch is also landed:

Gillnetting

A gill net is a curtain of netting that hangs in the water suspended from floats. Gill nets are almost invisible to marine life and rely on this fact to catch fish. The spaces in the net are designed to be big enough for the head of a fish to go through, but not its body. As the fish startles and backs out, its gills get caught in the net. Although gill nets are intended to catch certain species of fish, this fishing practice can result in a large quantity of bycatch.

Long-lining

Thousands of hooks all fish at once when a long-liner rolls out the gear. The central fishing line can be fifty miles long and strung with many smaller lines holding baited hooks. After leaving the lines to "soak" for a time to attract fish, long-line fishermen return to haul in their catch. Pelagic long-lining takes place near the sea surface, targeting midwater fish like swordfish and tuna. Demersal or "bottom" long-lining targets fish that live closer to the seafloor, like cod, halibut, and sablefish. Similar to gill nets, long-lines are intended to catch certain species of fish, but incidental species may also end up on the line.

Purse Seining

A purse seine is a large net that encircles a school of fish. The bottom of the net is strung with a line that the crew can pull closed. Small boats move out from a mother ship to surround the fish with netting, like cattle in a corral. The bottom of the net is then pulled closed. The baglike net then raises up, trapping the fish inside. Fishermen have traditionally used this method to capture sardines, herring, and mackerel, but purse seines are also used extensively for catching tuna. As imagined, when a giant net is pulled close, species other than those targeted may end up inside, resulting in bycatch.

Traps and Pots

Traps or "pots" are baited cages used to attract the catch and hold it alive until the fisherman returns. Often used for lobster, crab, and shrimp, traps are also occasionally used to catch bottom-dwelling fish, such as sablefish or West Coast rockfish.

Traps are made of wire or wood. They have an entrance, a "kitchen" chamber where the bait rests, and a "parlor" section where undersized animals can escape through vents. Trap fishermen usually lay out many traps attached in a line. After three or four days, they haul their pots aboard, releasing any animals that are too small, too large, or not the right species. Red rock crab, for example, that find their way into traps intended for more commercially viable species like Dungeness crab, are considered incidental catches.

Trawling/Dragging

Trawlers drag a cone-shaped net behind boats. Different types of trawl nets are used to fish in the midwater (pelagic trawling) and along the seafloor (bottom trawling). Pelagic trawling is often used to catch large schools of small fish such as anchovies; bottom trawlers target bottom-living fishes like cod, halibut, and rockfish. Some bottom trawl nets are fixed with chains that slap the seabed, "tickling" fish into the net above. "Rockhopper" trawls are fitted with heavy tires that roll the net along a rough and rocky seafloor. In dredging, a related form of fishing, nets with chain-mesh bottoms are dragged through soft sand to catch species like scallops. Unfortunately, trawlers are not selective when it comes to their nets being swept across the ocean floor, resulting in anything and everything being drawn inside, and often resulting in a large percentage of bycatch.

Trolling

Long rods pull fishing lines behind a moving vessel in the method known as trolling. Fishermen use a variety of lures and baits to troll for different fish at different depths. Trollers take speedy fish that will follow a moving lure, such as salmon, albacore tuna, and mahi-mahi. Even though trollers are targeting specific fish, other less desirable species may end up on the line, resulting in incidental catches.

PURCHASING, SELECTING & SEAFOOD CARE

Many people in this country, especially those not living on a coast, prefer to cook meat and poultry as their main sources of animal protein instead of fish. Some reasons for this include not knowing what kind of fish to buy or how to prepare it, or the belief that cooking fish can make a house smell fishy, or because the cook simply doesn't like fish. Yet, fish is so nutritious and heart-healthy. In fact, fish is more healthful than red meat and even poultry. Salmon, mackerel, bluefish, herring (all oily fish) are rich in omega-3 fatty acids believed to be both heart- and brain-healthy. The benefits of eating seafood have been proven by studies of fish-eating populations, especially those in Japan and Scandinavia. Eating fish also adds variety and interest to anyone's regular diet.

The following are some quick tips to help make buying and cooking fish and shellfish easier and more pleasant for the home cook:

Seafood Buying Tips

Fish and shellfish should always be purchased fresh or fresh-frozen. Although this may sound like an obvious statement, sometimes the supply chain takes too long to get fresh seafood to local stores, shortening its shelf life so that it appears unappetizing to the consumer. Frozen finned fish is a great alternative in this case. The first step is to ask questions. Learn about the various and unfamiliar species of bycatch being sold, which this book is intended to help you with. For the more ethically minded, learn the difference between seafood harvested in US waters and those brought in from

Fresh Skate Wing

overseas. All of this plays a vital role in purchasing the best and freshest seafood available. After receiving a little education, and now pointing to that delicious fish you are eager to prepare for your family and friends, refer to these helpful seafood-buying tips before you make the purchase:

- Seafood should never smell fishy. In fact, fresh fish should never have any unusual or offensive odor whatsoever. Always ask to smell the fish before you buy. Don't wait until you're home to discover the seafood you bought is spoiled. This tip refers to not only buying fresh fish, but all seafood, such as crab and scallops.

- If the fish you like has the head intact, take a moment and inspect the eyes, which should always be clear. Cloudy eyes are a sure sign the fish is not fresh or has been previously frozen. Same with the gills. They should be bright red. Pink or brown gills indicates a mishandled fish or one that has already spoiled.

- Inspect the flesh or meat. Fresh fish should be firm and spring back when touched. If your finger leaves an impression, the meat is soft and has probably spoiled.

- Examine the skin of the fish. The exterior should be clean, and if there are any fins intact, they should look crisp and moist, not discolored or dry, particularly around the edges.

- For species such as clams, crab, lobster, and the like, buy live whenever possible. This ensures the freshest quality rather than prepackaged products.

- When buying live shellfish like clams, mussels, and oysters, the shells should be tightly closed. If they are open, they should close when you touch them. They should also be housed in circulating seawater. If they are displayed on ice, make sure they are very cold—and alive.

- For live crab and lobster, they, too, should be stored in a circulating marine tank. These critters should be lively, especially when removed from the water. Do not purchase those that are limp and lifeless. If buying cooked crab or lobster, examine their shells. The exterior should be free of cracks and should smell clean and fresh.

Seafood Care

Seafood is different from other types of food because freshness is the key for safety and flavor. To ensure you and your family and friends will enjoy the best fish possible, remember these helpful pointers:

- If you find yourself purchasing frozen seafood, keep it frozen until you're ready to eat it. To properly thaw, defrost in the refrigerator and never at room temperature. Also, plan ahead, as you may need to defrost the day before your dinner party or family gathering.

- After purchasing your fresh seafood, it is best to remove the wrapping from the market and transfer the fish to an airtight container or to a plate covered with plastic wrap. If you are refrigerating more than one seafood, do not store them together in one container or plate, and do not let the juices from one seafood contact another seafood.

- Live seafood, like clams, crab, or lobster, cannot be frozen, but they should last for a couple of days if you keep them on ice in a cool dark place (note: do not cover the live seafood with ice, as marine seafood will quickly die in freshwater). Also remember that live seafood needs air to breathe, so remove them from the bag or container they were sold in.

- If traveling a good distance, have the supermarket or fishmonger add a bag of ice with your seafood purchase. Your fresh fish must stay cold if you want it to remain fresh.

If you are going to remember one rule when it comes to caring for your seafood, remember this one: Fresh seafood should always be consumed the day of purchase. The longer it sits, the quicker it spoils, as most fresh seafood has already been in transit four to six days before reaching the market.

Although we are introducing you to twenty-five kinds of bycatch, along with how to select and care for your purchase, keep in mind there are many other bycatch species out there for you to try. Feel free to experiment, try those other unusual fish, and see what you like best. But regardless of what you choose, always remember to buy from a reliable source, and always buy fresh whenever possible.

FISH MERCURY LEVEL INDEX

Eating seafood is good for you. Fish and shellfish contain vital nutrients, including omega-3 fatty acids, and are packed with protein, vitamins, and minerals such as iron. According to the FDA, the average American should consume two or three servings of fish per week, which can be eaten in place of other types of protein.

Sometimes, however, fish may contain a high level of mercury. If you're not familiar, mercury is an element collected in the ocean, which, in turn, is absorbed by fish, often becoming nothing more than a low-level neurotoxin. However, there are species prone to generating higher-levels of mercury that may cause serious health problems in people, particularly the nervous system in children and pregnant women.

Familiarize yourself with the mercury levels of the twenty-five fish featured in this cookbook. If you are pregnant or planning to become pregnant, it's a good idea for you to know what amount of fish sold in fish markets and restaurants is safe to eat.

There's really no limit to the amount of seafood you can consume in the LOW mercury level category. For those fish with MODERATE amounts of mercury, try and stick to six servings or fewer per month. Those HIGH in mercury should be consumed no more than three times per month.

HIGH in mercury

Amberjack

Bluefish

Cobia

Grouper

Mackerel (Spanish)

Marlin

Sea Bass

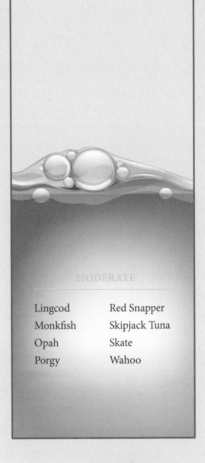

MODERATE

Lingcod	Red Snapper
Monkfish	Skipjack Tuna
Opah	Skate
Porgy	Wahoo

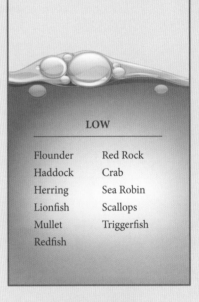

LOW

Flounder	Red Rock
Haddock	Crab
Herring	Sea Robin
Lionfish	Scallops
Mullet	Triggerfish
Redfish	

COOKING METHODS USED
IN THIS BOOK

Canning

We strongly suggest seeking out educational and instructional resources before practicing any form of preservation at home. Proper preservation of food has very specific needs that may result in food borne illnesses if not properly followed. Practice extreme caution and educate yourself in the control points necessary to ensure safety. That said, we thoroughly encourage the practice of preservation of seasonal ingredients to allow for usage and enjoyment throughout the entire year.

Deep-Frying

We like to use a solid vegetable shortening when deep-frying at the restaurant. Using a sturdy, heavy-bottomed pot or home deep-fryer is recommended, as well as always exercising extreme caution when working with hot oil. Handy tools to make your deep-frying experience great include a fine mesh skimmer, a draining rack, and a deep fat/candy thermometer. Drain fried product on a wire rack or absorbent paper towels, and always salt the finished product right when it comes out of the oil. Avoid introducing salt into the oil, which greatly decreases the oil's frying life.

Frying & Sautéing

While we will refer to various methods here, they may have some commonality and overlap, yet there are specific differences and details to consider when approaching as a cooking method.

When it comes to sautéing, ensure the ingredients have been "slacked" or tempered prior to cooking to allow the product to come up in temperature. This will provide for even cooking of the ingredient throughout. This may be more important to some ingredients than it is to others.

Thoroughly dry all ingredients using a kitchen towel or paper towel if necessary. Excess moisture on the product to be cooked will cause it to stick to the pan and may cause the ingredients to steam instead of sear.

Sautéing Example: Heat a large, heavy-bottomed sauté pan over medium heat until hot, about 3 or 4 minutes. Add enough oil to just coat the bottom of the sauté pan. Heat the oil for 15 to 30 seconds before introducing the fish. Place the fish into the pan away from you while taking extreme care as you introduce each piece. Cook the fish until the bottom is golden brown and the fish releases easily from the pan. If fish seems to stick, it may need a short time longer. Moderate your heat throughout the cooking process to ensure a moderate cooking of the fish. Searing the first side should take roughly 1 or 2 minutes. Carefully slide your fish spatula under the fish and flip to cook remaining side. Introduce butter into the sauté pan and allow for the butter to melt. The moisture in the butter may spatter and pop slightly. As the fish cooks on the second side, using a large metal spoon, tilt the pan to allow for the butter to collect on one side; collect the butter with the spoon and baste the fish with the hot butter. Continue this basting throughout the remaining cooking time. Allow for caramelization of the fish and remove from heat when color has turned opaque throughout and the flesh feels firm across entire piece. Remove and sprinkle with coarse flake salt after placing onto wire rack or paper towel–lined plate to rest.

Find a high-quality oil or blend that will allow for high-heat applications and should have a smoke point of at least 500°F. Using the wrong oil for high-heat cooking will cause the food to have off flavors and may be a safety hazard.

It is imperative that you use an adequately large sauté pan when searing fish or other ingredients at high heat and that you do not overcrowd the pan. You must provide an adequate amount of space between the individual pieces to ensure a consistent temperature of the pan. Each addition of fish and other ingredients will in effect remove energy, cool the pan, and drop the temperature of the sauté pan as it responds to the cold temperature of the fish. Overcrowding the pan will cause the temperature to drop excessively and result in the fish sticking and subsequently steaming instead of searing.

Grilling

While we ultimately recommend natural hardwood lump charcoal for grilling, natural gas or propane will work as an alternative method. We also recommend using a chimney when heating hardwood charcoal. Be sure to thoroughly clean and treat the cooking grates, as any residual carbon may cause tearing or damage to the fish during cookery. Also, be sure the grill grates over the coals are well oiled and extremely hot. The opportunity for the fish to be unmanageable or sticking is greatly reduced by increased heat at the cooking surface and a properly oiled grill. We also use a rag, rolled tightly into a cylinder (tied tight with butchers' twine) and dipped in clean oil (vegetable or canola) to season the hot grill grates with a pair of tongs just prior to cooking. To prepare fish for cooking, make sure that it has been thoroughly dried and well-oiled to prevent it from sticking to the grates. There are many products available to facilitate cooking seafood on a grill and, while they may be successful, following the steps listed above will yield just as successful, and likely a better, result.

Roasting

Roasting allows for an intense caramelization, increased browning (Maillard reaction), and flavor development because of a dry, indirect, often high-heat cooking environment.

Our general method for facilitating the roasting process is done using our wood-fired oven, ranging from temperatures of 700°F to 900°F. Nothing can match the cooking processes that occur within. However, when roasting fish or vegetables in a conventional oven, we always do so at temperatures ranging from 425°F to 500°F, applying a constant focus to the product, and rotating or turning often to ensure uniform results. While roasting is often used for cooking meats, seafood, and vegetables at lower temperatures for longer periods of time, the inclusions of the roasting process present in this guide are generally higher heat for shorter periods, with an emphasis on the characteristics listed at the top of this section.

When roasting at home, be sure to preheat your oven thoroughly at least 30 minutes prior to cooking (times may vary depending on the specifics of your equipment). The addition of thermal mass inside your oven will increase your results dramatically. For example, add a large ceramic "pizza stone" or high-heat tolerable food-specific oven bricks, of significant size and thickness. We also recommend finishing off the higher-heat referenced roasting processes by introducing your product to the broiler just prior to finishing to boost the overall caramelization and high-heat needs of the cooking process.

Smoking

Everything we smoke at Salt of the Earth is done using traditional methods: utilizing an offset fire box for indirect heat and constant monitoring of temperatures at various points throughout the smoking chamber. While many pieces of equipment are available that control much of the cooking process present in smoking, thus eliminating the need for intensive involvement from the cook, we celebrate and demand the interaction and challenge presented from the classical methods developed with our historic food cultures in an effort to enact preservation and provide nourishment and food sources throughout the seasons in which food was less abundant or difficult to procure. True American barbecue is an art and always the result of time and experience.

We use almost exclusively white oak for smoking, apart from the moments that benefit from tossing a bourbon barrel stave onto the fire. For most seafood, use a very mild wood. In addition to white oak, apple or pecan wood would also be appropriate.

The most important aspect of this method is "temperature and consistency." Creating and maintaining a consistent temperature of 225°F to 250°F is imperative. If the opportunity for a cold smoke (largely reliant on available equipment) exists, it would be ideal in many applications. When placing product onto the smoker, ensure it is located as far away from the heat source as possible. We like to bring the smoker up to cooking temperature for at least 30 minutes before placing any product on it; this helps ensure you can maintain a consistent temperature environment.

Sous-Vide

At the restaurant, we greatly utilize the technology of thermal immersion circulators (see Anova in the Resource section, page 175) combined with a vacuum sealed product cooked in a water bath, commonly known as Sous Vide (under pressure). This incredibly gentle and consistent cooking method allows for an unmatched ability to control the flavor and texture of the final product. We utilize our "oven aquatic" or "the wet oven" for virtually everything we poach, and as a foundational cooking step when preparing much of the vegetables we serve throughout every season.

While we've been relishing in the dramatic results achieved through this method for many years, the equipment and resources necessary for home application have recently become readily available and reasonably priced, with many products now available online. Sous Vide cooking is dramatically more present in the home kitchen than ever before. A great deal of resources exist to guide the home cook to master this virtually simple and basic method that functions based on the balance of two factors: time and temperature.

We generally like to start the circulator 10 degrees higher than the desired cooking temperature, as the introduction of the product into the water bath will cause the bath's temperature to react, and inconsistent results may occur as a result. Start your bath temperature a bit higher than you intend to cook, and then adjust the thermal settings on your device. The specific temperature fluctuation you may experience will be dependent on many factors present with your specific setup, and the specifics listed above are simply provided for perspective of how we approach the cooking method here at the restaurant. Trial and error, experience, and perspective will provide the knowledge necessary to master this technique.

KITCHEN TOOLS & EQUIPMENT

Cooking Thermometer

A well-calibrated and accurate thermometer is a foundational necessity for every kitchen and every cook. Largely available and reasonably affordable, the consistent usage of this tool will allow for a deeper understanding and correlation to specific points of control throughout various cooking processes. While cooking is largely intuitive, a scientific approach and calculated evaluations will always provide a consistent result. In the restaurant, we use a variety of types of thermometers, but most often rely on a simple and relatively inexpensive digital instant-read pocket thermometer. High heat deep-frying on the stovetop can benefit from the use of a probe style or stationary candy thermometer to provide a constant read out of temperature and greatly increase safety in a safety-concerning environment. Be sure to calibrate frequently, utilizing online resources or manufacturers, guidelines to facilitate this process.

Deep-Fryer

Where many deep-frying needs can be facilitated using an appropriately sized pot and a carefully executed heating application, a dedicated deep-fryer can be a game changer, especially when preparing multiple elements that have to come together at once.

Sea Robins, Triggerfish & Other Overlooked Seafood

Food Processor

While not a necessity in the home kitchen, food processors are a great tool for making quick work of what were once arduous tasks, such as whisking mayonnaise. It also comes with attachments that can quickly grate hard cheeses or process vegetables for soup.

Immersion Blender

Also known as a "stick blender," a solid immersion blender can greatly increase the efficient use of your time for many cooking applications. Allowing for the processing of large batches of cooked products directly in their cooking vessels, eliminating the need for transferring hot food to alternate pieces of equipment, an immersion blender is an incredibly helpful option in many instances. When the final texture of ingredients is of strong concern or necessity, an immersion blender may not be the best option, as it often lacks the ability to achieve a super fine and superiorly smooth texture that you would experience from a traditional blender.

Kitchen Blender

A strong blender is one of the most important kitchen tools for a serious home cook. Responsible for the final texture of any puréed cooked or raw ingredient, as well as a strong mechanical option for building emulsifications. A category that is well worth a serious investment, the right selection of equipment will provide a long-term quality addition to your countertop. The KitchenAid ProLine blender and the newly released KitchenAid Commercial series blender are honestly the most amazing pieces of equipment I've ever had the opportunity to work with. I use these incredibly functional and well-built machines in our professional kitchens and in my home.

Thermal Immersion Circulator

See Sous Vide, listed in Cooking Methods.

Vacuum Sealer

Quite specifically, this is a kitchen tool that utilizes specialized bags to eliminate oxygen from an ingredient and seals the bag to maintain the oxygen-reduced or-eliminated environment. Vacuum sealers are essential for sous vide cooking methods and provide a great deal of value in allowing for preservation of ingredients by eliminating one factor that causes ingredient decay and spoilage. We use "ROP" or "Reduced Oxygen Packaging" to quickly facilitate pickling, brining, and marinating when time is not an option for the natural processes to occur. By eliminating the oxygen present in an environment and ingredient, the additions to the vacuum bag (often aromatics, brines, and marinades) are forced into the ingredient, quickly facilitating processes that would take significantly longer periods of time.

When purchasing bycatch, nowhere is freshness more paramount. Developing a relationship with your local fishmonger is essential to serving great seafood dishes.

FIRST COURSES & SMALL BITES

Pickled Herring   2

Butter Poached Monkfish Cocktail   6

Red Rock Crab Cake with Roasted Pepper Mustard
and Baby Kale   9

Korean Fried Skate Wings   12

Coconut Grilled Wahoo   14

PICKLED HERRING

MAKES 1 (2-QUART) JARS

ALTERNATIVE FISH: MACKEREL, SHAD, SMELT

While my experience with pickled herring was always limited to a jar or two in Grandma's fridge, my mother, Ingrid Markstrom, speaks of her travels to Sweden at a young age. She would spend her college summers in Stockholm visiting and traveling with her cousin, Ingmar, and other family members who lived throughout the country. Pickled herring, accompanied by wasa bröd (hard tack or thin cracker) and butter, was served at every table, often at every meal, and always at breakfast. Our preparation varies slightly from the traditional experience that my mother regularly enjoyed.

Herring

There are more than 180 species in the herring family, including sardines and anchovies. The Guinness Book of World Records *states that the Atlantic herring is considered the world's most numerous fish. When herring migrate, they can run in schools extending 17 miles and containing millions of fish.*

The Atlantic herring, in particular, is a small plankton-feeder that grows to a maximum of 17 inches and 1.5 pounds. They are an abundant, pelagic fish that inhabit the open sea and offshore banks for most of their lives. However, in the spring and summer, young juveniles are numerous in inshore waters along the Maine coast. Adults migrate across hundreds of miles of ocean during their life spans. In the winter, schools of migrating Atlantic herring can join forces, forming massive expanses of fish stretching as far as the eye can see.

Just as marine birds and mammals have taken advantage of bountiful herring schools along northern coasts, humans have long depended upon this resource for sustenance. Nearly every culture along North Atlantic coasts, from historical tribes and settlements to modern communities, have fished for herring, which are often an incidental catch when targeting sardines and anchovies.

Today, in the Gulf of Maine, herring are harvested primarily by purse

2 large fresh herring fillets (20–24 ounces), cleaned and trimmed

½ cup fine sea salt

Milk, as needed

1⅓ cups sugar

1 cup white vinegar

1 cup cold water

24 whole black peppercorns

20 allspice berries

20 whole cloves

12 fresh laurel leaves (or bay leaves)

3 small red onions, peeled and thinly sliced

2 medium-size carrots, peeled and sliced into thin coins

Place the fresh herring into a wide container, and apply the salt liberally. Allow to sit covered overnight in the refrigerator. The next day, remove the fish, rinse off the salt, and place into a shallow container. Add the milk to the fillets just to cover. Allow to sit for 4 to 6 hours. Remove the fish from the milk mixture and rinse lightly with water. Set aside.

In a 2-quart saucepan over medium-high heat, add the sugar, vinegar, and cold water. Bring to a boil and boil until the sugar is dissolved, about 1 or 2 minutes. Remove from heat and stir in the peppercorns, allspice, cloves, laurel leaves, sliced onions, and carrots. Let cool. Add the herring and cover with plastic wrap. Chill for at least 72 hours.

Note: If intended for storage, assemble the soaked herring (sliced on a diagonal ½- to 1-inch thick) into sterilized quart mason jars, sprinkling in the aromatics from the brine as you fill the jars. Pour the cooled brine over the fish to cover, seal, and store.

seiners and mid-water trawlers that
also fish for sardines and anchovies.

*The sardine canneries in Maine,
New Brunswick, and most of the
North Atlantic states exclusively
process young Atlantic herring.
In other locations, however, a can
labeled "sardines" may contain
an entirely different type of fish.
The Pacific sardine (Sardinops
sagax), or pilchard, is the fish that
inspired Cannery Row in Monterey,
California—immortalized by
American writer John Steinbeck.
While the fish share the same family
and sometimes the same name on a
can label, Atlantic herring and Pacific
sardines are two distinct species.*

To Serve: Remove the herring from the brine, and pat dry with paper towels to
remove any excess moisture. Slice into portions, cutting the fish on the diagonal.
Pile the fish onto a dish, and serve with Pickled Beets (page 165), Linnea's Sweet
Pickles (page 162), and Dill Cream (page 155).

Suggested Pairing

Premier Cru Chablis, Burgundy, France

Chablis is located in the northernmost winemaking region in Burgundy,
France. The area, spurred by limestone soil that contains deposits of
fossilized oyster shells, produces some of the most unique chardonnay
in the world. Ripe, floral, and round, this wine lends its salinity, drawn
from the soil, to be a great partner in the marriage of the brininess in
pickled fish and the richness of a cream sauce.

BUTTER POACHED MONKFISH COCKTAIL

Serves 12
Alternative fish: grouper, halibut, sea bass, sea robin, snapper

This is a very simple interpretation of the classic first course often celebrated with seafood and frequently found at formal gatherings. We utilize monkfish to mirror the texture associated with the flavors of this dish, which is commonly presented with some form of shrimp.

At the restaurant, we greatly utilize the technology of thermal immersion circulators combined with a vacuum-sealed product cooked in a water bath, commonly known as Sous Vide (under pressure). This incredibly gentle and consistent cooking method allows for an unmatched ability to control the flavor and texture of the final product. We utilize our "oven aquatic" or "the wet oven" for virtually everything we poach. While we've been relishing in the dramatic results achieved through this method for many years, the equipment and resources necessary for home application have recently become readily available and reasonably priced, with many products now available online.

Monkfish

Clearly, the monkfish won't win any beauty contests, but it does receive high praise in many culinary circles because of its sweet, meaty flesh and firm, oily texture.

With its large, flat head and wide mouth lined with needle like teeth, the rather ugly-looking monkfish, sometimes referred to as goosefish, is often found sitting on the bottom of the ocean floor where it lies in wait to consume unwary prey that can be the same size as the monkfish itself.

At just over about three feet in length and averaging around eight to twelve pounds, the monkfish is common along the coasts of Europe as well as North America, the Mediterranean, China, and Japan. It is here where commercial fishermen, often dragging their gill or trawl nets near or along the ocean floor in search of more desirable species, encounter this extraordinary sea dweller. In the United States, most monkfish are pulled from the waters off Massachusetts, New Jersey, Rhode Island, and New York.

Only the monkfish tail is edible, and the lean, white tail meat is sold whole or filleted.

Horseradish Cream
10 ounces sour cream

2 tablespoons horseradish, finely grated (using a microplane)

4 ounces cream cheese

1½ ounces cultured buttermilk

1 teaspoon white wine vinegar

1 teaspoon lemon juice

Sea salt, to taste

Smoked Tomato Purée
2 tablespoons vegetable oil

1 small yellow onion, peeled and diced

2 tablespoons fresh lemon juice

1 teaspoon chili powder

1 teaspoon sweet paprika

1 teaspoon smoked paprika

1 teaspoon coriander seed, toasted

1 pinch celery seed

¼ cup apple cider vinegar

16 ounces whole canned tomatoes in juice

2 tablespoons tomato paste

1 teaspoon all-natural hickory smoke powder

Sea salt, to taste

Spicy Lemon Curd
12 egg yolks

½ cup granulated sugar

½ cup brown sugar

1 cup fresh lemon juice

1 teaspoon red chili flakes

1 cup unsalted butter, cut into cubes

Butter Poached Monkfish
6 monkfish fillets (about 6 ounces each), cleaned and trimmed

½ pound butter

6 garlic cloves, smashed and peeled

18 whole black peppercorns, toasted and crushed

4 fresh laurel leaves (or 2 dried bay leaves)

4 sprigs fresh thyme

12 Caramelized Lemon slices (page 130)

1 large bunch arugula (or other hearty green)

Olive oil, as needed

Smoked sea salt, as needed

To make the Horseradish Cream:

In a large mixing bowl, whisk together the sour cream, horseradish, cream cheese, buttermilk, vinegar, and lemon juice until well combined. Season to taste with sea salt.

To make the Smoked Tomato:

In a medium stockpot, heat the vegetable oil over low heat. Add the onion and cook, stirring occasionally, until onion begins to caramelize, about 15 to 20 minutes. Add the lemon juice and cook until the juice has completely reduced and sugars have caramelized. Add the chili powder, both paprikas, coriander, and celery seeds, and cook for 1 minute. Deglaze the pot with the apple cider vinegar and reduce by half. Add the tomatoes and tomato paste, and simmer until reduced again by half. Add the hickory smoke powder. Remove from the heat, and place mixture into a blender, taking care to only fill the blender halfway with the mixture. Purée until smooth and season to taste with sea salt.

To make the Spicy Lemon Curd:

Add about 2 inches of water to a medium saucepot. Place over medium-low heat. In a large mixing bowl, whisk the eggs, sugars, lemon juice, and chili flakes. Place the mixing bowl over the pot (also called a double boiler, which allows for gentle cooking). Whisking frequently, heat the egg mixture until thickened (188°F), about 8 to 10 minutes. Slowly whisk in the butter cubes a few at a time, making sure the butter is completely incorporated before the next addition. Remove from the heat and cool. To store the curd, place into a container and press a piece of plastic wrap against the surface of the curd to inhibit a skin forming.

To make the Butter Poached Monkfish:

Divide the monkfish fillets, butter, garlic, pepper, laurel leaves, thyme, and Caramelized Lemon slices equally into cryo-vac or vacuum bags. Do not fill bags more than halfway. Seal the contents.

Set your home Thermal Immersion Circulator temperature to 145°F.

Prepare the water bath and ensure the temperature of the water is fully achieved prior to introduction of the bags. Place the sealed bags into the water bath; they should be fully submerged. Lower the temperature of the circulator to 135°F, and set the timer for 22 minutes. Remove the sealed bags from the water bath and place immediately into an ice water bath to cool.

To Serve: Dress the greens well with olive oil, and sprinkle with smoked sea salt. Place the greens onto a serving platter in mounds across area of the plate. Place the Smoked Tomato Purée into a squeeze bottle or, using a small spoon, decorate around the plate with dollops of the purée.

Continued on page 8

Gently remove the fish from the sealed bags, discarding the other ingredients, and peeling away any fat that may be adhered to the fish. Gently wipe the fish clean with paper towels, place on cutting board, and carefully slice into ½-inch-thick pieces.

Assemble the monkfish across the platter, over and around the dressed arugula and purée. Finish the plate with dollops of the Horseradish Cream, and sprinkle with a bit of smoked sea salt. Place the Spicy Lemon Curd into a squeeze bottle, and garnish the fish and plate with small rounds varied in size throughout.

SUGGESTED PAIRING:

Gavi di Gavi, Piemonte, Italy

Gavi di Gavi wine is produced from the Cortese grape grown in Northeast Italy. Gavi has produced wine since the seventeenth century and serves as an everyday drinking "bianco" for most Italians. Its unassuming flavor is usually fruity, dry, and balanced. A welcome match for the meaty but tender texture of monkfish or lobster.

RED ROCK CRAB CAKE WITH ROASTED PEPPER MUSTARD AND BABY KALE

SERVES 6

ALTERNATIVE FISH: BLUE CRAB, DUNGENESS CRAB, HIGH-QUALITY LUMP CRABMEAT

We rarely offer crab cakes in our restaurant, as they're often found on many restaurant menus, but I absolutely love to prepare this recipe at home, especially for breakfast—they're a perfect accompaniment to fried eggs. The Roasted Pepper Mustard featured in this dish can easily be substituted with any of the delicious creamy sauces found in the Recipe Foundations chapter (page 141), such as Spicy Mayonnaise or the Confit Garlic Shallot Mayonnaise (page 163).

RED ROCK CRAB

The red rock crab, which is larger than a blue crab but smaller than a Dungeness crab, are very common in the cold waters of the Pacific Northwest. They are frequently an incidental catch for commercial crabbers targeting the highly prized Dungeness crab. Despite rock crabs preferring a rockier substrate as opposed to sandy bottoms for the Dungeness, both crabs are often found foraging in the same environment, and both will enter baited commercial crab pots with ease.

The red rock crab can easily be distinguished from other crabs by their deep red color and the black tips on their claws. Their name derives from their extremely thick shell, which is difficult to break. Red rock crabs are also quite aggressive.

Because red rock crabs aren't as meaty and sought-after as other crabs, such as the Dungeness, they are typically not found in supermarkets or seafood shops. However, red rock crab meat is mild and tasty, with most of the meat found in the claws and thigh areas.

CRAB CAKES

2 pounds fresh rock crabmeat

2 farm-fresh pastured eggs, lightly blended

½ cup Fresh Breadcrumbs (page 156)

1 tablespoon garlic, peeled and minced

1 tablespoon shallot, peeled and minced

¼ teaspoon black peppercorns, cracked or coarsely milled

2 tablespoons Roasted Pepper Mustard (page 171), plus more for serving

2 teaspoons kosher salt

1 tablespoon finely minced flat-leaf parsley

FOR FRYING:

3 cups Fresh Breadcrumbs (page 156)

2 tablespoons olive oil

½ stick salted butter

Smoked sea salt or coarse flake salt, as needed

DRESSED BABY KALE

½ pound baby kale (or fine chiffonade of mature kale)

High-quality olive oil, as needed

½ fresh squeezed lemon

Sea salt, to taste

TO MAKE THE CRAB CAKES:

Separate the crabmeat into two equal portions. Set one portion aside.

In a medium-size mixing bowl, combine the first portion of the crabmeat along with the eggs, Fresh Breadcrumbs, garlic, shallot, pepper, Roasted Pepper Mustard, salt, and parsley. Fold gently, ensuring ingredients are well combined. Carefully fold in the remaining crabmeat, using care to preserve the larger pieces. Refrigerate for at least 1 hour. (Note: If intending on assembling as a part of breakfast, prepare the mixture the night before, covering with plastic wrap before storing in the refrigerator.)

Divide the mixture into 6 equal portions (roughly one heaping ½ cup), but do not overwork the mix. Pack each portion tightly together using both hands, forming a sphere. Place each portion of crab mixture directly into the breadcrumbs, which have been placed in a shallow container. Press the ball into

Continued on page 10

the breadcrumbs, scoop the breadcrumbs around the crab ball to cover, and press gently into a patty, using your hands to support and firmly press the edges into shape. Cover each patty with an additional scoop of breadcrumbs and set aside as you continue the process with the remaining portions.

Heat a large sauté pan over moderate heat. Add the olive oil and butter and allow to heat. Gently place the crab cakes into the pan and fry until crispy and golden brown. Carefully flip each cake, taking care to not break them. Once the crab cakes have been fully cooked on both sides, remove and transfer to a plate lined with paper towels, and sprinkle with smoked sea salt or coarse flake salt.

To make the Dressed Baby Kale:

In a small mixing bowl, dress the kale with a little olive oil and fresh lemon juice, and season to taste with sea salt.

To Serve: Take a heaping spoonful of the Roasted Pepper Mustard and smear across the plate. Place a warm crab cake off-center of the plate, and place a pile of the Dressed Baby Kale beside the crab cake. Serve with a dish of additional Roasted Pepper Mustard, as this dipping sauce is highly addictive.

Suggested Pairing

Pinot Gris, Columbia Valley, Washington

Located at the same latitude as Burgundy and Bordeaux, Washington state produces more wine than any other state except California. Most vineyards are located on the warm and arid eastern side of the state. These conditions create crisp, acid-driven wines with flavors of pear and apple. This vibrant style of wine lends in pairing with seafood of all textures and flavor profiles.

KOREAN FRIED SKATE WINGS

SERVES 4

ALTERNATIVE FISH: HADDOCK, FLOUNDER, SANDDABS, SOLE

Jeff Bailey, the opening chef at our second restaurant, and I developed this recipe from a popular chicken wing dish. The Ramen Noodle Dredge and addictive Korean BBQ Sauce that follows are a perfect combination with skate wings as the featured protein. You'll never go back to chicken wings after enjoying this flavorful dish.

SKATE

There are roughly one hundred species of skate worldwide. Not to be confused with rays, skate are flat, diamond-shaped fish that patrol the ocean floor with their mouths on the underside of their body. Like sharks, skates are comprised of cartilage and do not contain a bony skeleton. Skates also have large fins resembling wings, which is the edible portion of the animal.

Skates are a common bycatch of commercial fishermen using bottom trawls or bottom gill nets to target other ground species, especially in the US Atlantic.

When purchasing skate, try and find longnose or big skates caught on the west coast of the United States or winter skates caught in the Atlantic. These are more sustainable than, say, longnose skate from the Canadian waters of British Columbia.

Fresh skate meat, which is rather inexpensive compared to other seafood, is beautiful in appearance with its shiny, pink fan like ribs and is super tender and mild tasting, which is distinctive to the fish. However, be aware that sometimes fresh skate meat can be tough, and it does go bad quickly. If the meat ever has the faintest smell of ammonia, do not buy or discard. This is usually a sign of inferior, improper handling of the meat.

KOREAN BBQ SAUCE
Makes 4 cups

1 cup Gochugaru chili flakes*

½ cup + 2 tablespoons Hoisin sauce

½ cup ketchup

¾ cup honey

½ cup sake

2 tablespoons rice wine vinegar

¼ cup finely grated fresh ginger

2 tablespoons finely grated garlic

½ cup soy sauce

RAMEN NOODLE DREDGE
3 packages Ramen noodles

1 reserved Ramen noodle seasoning packet

½ cup cornstarch

¼ cup rice flour

3 cups cultured buttermilk

SKATE
4 (6-ounce) skate fillets, skin removed

Kosher salt, as needed

Granulated sugar, as needed

Cooking oil (e.g., vegetable, avocado, grapeseed)

1 reserved Ramen noodle seasoning packet or fine sea salt

*This floral and slightly sweet Korean chili is an absolute staple for your spice shelf. If unavailable, simply substitute with red chili flakes (reducing the measurement to ¼ cup).

TO MAKE THE KOREAN BBQ SAUCE:

In a small saucepot over medium heat, combine the chili flakes, Hoisin sauce, ketchup, honey, sake, vinegar, ginger, garlic, and soy sauce. Bring to a boil, whisking throughout. Immediately remove from heat. Allow to cool and reserve until ready to use.

TO MAKE THE RAMEN NOODLE DREDGE:

Crush the dry Ramen noodles into small pieces and place into a blender. Process the noodles to a fine powder. Season the powder with 1 packet of the Ramen seasoning blend, and mix well with the cornstarch and rice flour. Transfer the mixture to a wide, shallow container. Use a similar container for the buttermilk.

To make the Skate:

Cut each skate fillet into 3 or 4 pieces.

Pat the skate dry with a kitchen towel or paper towels. Season the skate (thoroughly but not excessively) with a 50/50 mixture of the kosher salt and granulated sugar. Place the skate into an appropriately sized dish and place in refrigerator for 1 hour.

Remove the skate from the refrigerator 30 minutes prior to cooking to allow the fish to come up in temperature. This will provide for even cooking. Pat the skate dry using a kitchen towel or paper towel. Excess moisture on the fish will cause it to stick to the pan and may cause the fish to steam instead of sear.

Place each piece of skate into the buttermilk, coating well, and then dredge in the Ramen Noodle Dredge, ensuring a thorough coating. Repeat this process with all remaining portions of skate wing.

Heat a large sauté pan over medium heat. Add the oil, and carefully place a skate wing in the pan. Cook until golden brown. Using a fish spatula, carefully turn the skate wing and cook on opposite side until also golden brown and fish is cooked through. Transfer to a plate lined with paper towels and season the skate with some Ramen noodle seasoning or fine sea salt. Repeat with the remaining fillets.

To Serve: Assemble the crispy skate wing pieces on brown paper or a large serving platter. Serve with a side of the Korean BBQ Sauce. Be prepared to refill the Korean BBQ Sauce, as we find it to be insanely addictive.

Suggested Pairing

Kabinett Riesling, Mosel, Germany

Germany offers a luxury that no other wine-producing region affords: labels indicating not only varietal but ripeness and sweetness. Kabinett is the ripest on the spectrum, revealing delicate fruit flavors, bracing acid, and lasting mineral notes that carry a lengthy finish. Find success in matching this wine with fried and spicy foods.

COCONUT GRILLED WAHOO

Serves 4 to 6
Alternative fish: albacore

While we ultimately recommend natural hardwood lump charcoal for grilling, natural gas or propane will work, too. We also recommend using a chimney when heating hardwood charcoal. Always clean the grilling grates, as any residual carbon may cause tearing or damage to the fish during cooking, and make sure the grates are well-oiled and extremely hot. The risk of sticking is greatly reduced by increased heat at the cooking surface and a properly oiled grill. Use a rag, rolled tightly into a cylinder (tied with butchers' twine) and dipped in clean oil (vegetable or canola) to season the hot grill grates with a pair of tongs just prior to cooking. As for the Toasted Coconut Cream in this delicious dish, we developed this method of infusing and reducing coconut milk into a thickened sauce for a pastry application. The opportunity to repurpose and refocus the method of intensifying the flavor of coconut is perfectly represented with seafood. Balance the sweetness and acidity to your desires. Meanwhile, the Pow-Pow Sauce packs a punch. For the Roasted Pineapple, you can also roast next to the coals. For the adventurous, save the preparation as a final step and roast over the charcoal once the fish has been removed.

Wahoo

Wahoo (referred to as Ono in Hawaii; meaning "good to eat") is a close relative of the king mackerel. They are slender, pelagic fish with finely serrated, triangular teeth and beak like snouts. They are distributed worldwide in tropical and subtropical waters.

The wahoo, like other pelagics, tend to live alone or form small, loose groups. They like to congregate near drifting objects and move with the changing seasons, traveling into cooler waters during warm summer months. Wahoo feed on a variety of fish, as well as squid. They have been recorded swimming in short bursts of up to 50 miles per hour, allowing for quick capture of prey species. Wahoo may grow to more than 100 pounds, but the usual size of a Hawaiian wahoo is 8 to 30 pounds.

About half of the commercial wahoo landed in Hawaii are caught by trollers. The remainder are caught incidentally on long-line gear targeted for tuna. Troll-caught and long-line wahoo are marketed through fish auctions in Honolulu and Hilo, where much of the catch is shipped directly to restaurants in Hawaii and the US mainland.

Toasted Coconut Cream

14 ounces unsweetened shredded coconut

5 (14-ounce) cans unsweetened coconut milk

2 tablespoons whole coriander seed, toasted

¼ vanilla bean, split and scraped

1 lime, juiced

Sea salt, as needed

3 or 4 tablespoons dark brown sugar

Pow-Pow Sauce

2 ounces sesame oil

1 small onion, peeled and diced

2 stalks lemongrass, sliced thinly

2 tablespoons minced ginger

6 garlic cloves, smashed and peeled

2 tablespoons toasted coriander seed

1 teaspoon toasted cardamom seed

2 tablespoons sweet paprika

1 cup white distilled vinegar

2 cups sweet chili sauce

2 cups ketchup

2–8 tablespoons fermented chili sauce, depending on your desired heat level

Roasted Pineapple

1 pineapple, cored and cut lengthwise into 8 even pieces

Neutral-flavored cooking oil (grapeseed or canola), as needed

10 Confit Garlic Cloves (page 151) or fresh garlic, smashed and peeled

½ teaspoon Gochugaru chili powder

2 tablespoons coconut sap sugar (or dark brown sugar)

Kosher salt, to taste

1 lime, juiced

¼ cup fresh cilantro leaves, minced

Grilled Wahoo

4 cups water

4 tablespoons salt

3 tablespoons brown sugar

12 ounces pineapple juice

1 grapefruit, juiced

1 bunch cilantro leaves, torn

2 tablespoons whole coriander seed, toasted

3 pounds fresh wahoo fillets, cleaned and trimmed

To make the Toasted Coconut Cream:

In a heavy-bottomed pot over low heat, add the shredded coconut. Cook until the coconut is golden brown and toasted, stirring constantly. Add the coconut milk, coriander seed, and vanilla bean. Bring to a boil, and reduce to a simmer, stirring often, and cook until reduced by two-thirds in volume and noticeably thicker. Strain and season with the lime juice, salt, and some brown sugar.

To make the Pow-Pow Sauce:

In a large heavy-bottomed pot, heat the sesame oil over medium heat. Add the onion, lemongrass, ginger, and garlic. Sweat until softened, about 2 or 3 minutes. Add the coriander and cardamom seeds, along with the sweet paprika. Cook 1 or 2 minutes, or until fragrant. Add the vinegar, chili sauce, ketchup, and fermented chili sauce. Simmer over medium-low heat until slightly reduced. Strain and reserve.

To make the Roasted Pineapple:

Preheat the oven to 400°F.

Coat the pineapple lightly with oil, along with the garlic, and place onto a baking sheet. Sprinkle with the chili powder and sugar. Roast the pineapple until golden brown, roughly 15 to 18 minutes. Remove from oven and allow to cool slightly. Place into a medium-size mixing bowl and crush well, incorporating all the ingredients. Season with a dash of salt and the lime juice. Add the minced cilantro and reserve.

To make the Grilled Wahoo:

In a saucepot over medium heat, add the water, salt, and brown sugar, and stir until dissolved. Remove from heat and cool. Add the pineapple juice, grapefruit juice, cilantro, and coriander seed, and stir well to combine.

Place the wahoo fillets into a large non-reactive dish, and cover with the marinade. Marinate the fish at room temperature for at least 30 minutes. If not cooking right away, remove the fish from the marinade and reserve in the refrigerator until ready to cook. Note: Allow the refrigerated fish to come up to temperature before cooking.

Remove the fish from the marinade and dry thoroughly before proceeding.

Prepare an outdoor grill at high heat. Place the fish directly over the hot coals or grill and cook for roughly 3 minutes, turning the fish as needed. If necessary,

Continued on page 16

finish cooking by transferring the fish to a location on the grill away from the direct heat source and cover with the grill lid (for tips on grilling, see page xxxi). Remove the fish from the grill, and allow to rest for 5 to 10 minutes. Slice the fish into 1-inch portions, and prepare for the serving platter.

TO SERVE: Add a large dollop of the Toasted Coconut Cream to the platter, and spread it in an artistic fashion. Spoon portions of Roasted Pineapple in a similar fashion. Place the wahoo portions in a similar manner. With enthusiasm and energy, spoon the Pow-Pow Sauce over the platter and fish.

SUGGESTED PAIRING:

Chardonnay, Margaret River, Australia

Sitting on the beautiful and sparsely inhabited Western coast of Australia, Margaret River teems with wild landscape and remarkable wines. Its chardonnays can ripen early and run the span from crisp to creamy. Winds off the Indian Ocean keep the summer cool and the influx of seafood readily available. Its wines are a natural partner with grilled fish and vegetable preparations.

SALADS & RAW

Grilled Marlin with Spring "Panzanella"   20

Opah Crudo   24

Scallop Aguachile   29

Red Rock Crab Salad   34

Olive Oil Poached Skipjack Tuna & Green Bean
"Niçoise" Salad   36

Chilled Poached Triggerfish, Savory Granola
& Green Smoothie Broth   40

GRILLED MARLIN WITH SPRING "PANZANELLA"

SERVES 4 TO 6

ALTERNATIVE FISH: SALMON, SWORDFISH, TUNA

The ramp, a wild spring leek, is one of the first green seasonal ingredients we experience after a long, cold winter filled with beets and the cellared root vegetables that made it to spring. We procure ramps from a variety of sources, as we encourage a sustainable harvest from the wild patches that grow throughout the Allegan County and beyond. With an incredibly short window of availability, we process, serve, and preserve roughly three to four hundred pounds of ramps in a two- to three-week period. Meanwhile, the marinade we make and the robust flavors presented in the "Panzanella Salad" pair perfectly with the meaty texture of the marlin.

MARLIN

Native to the tropical and temperate waters of the Atlantic, Pacific, and Indian Oceans, marlin, with its sliver-blue color, pronounced dorsal fin, and long, lethal, spear-shaped upper jaw, is considered one of the largest and most beautiful fish in the ocean. It is also one of the fastest fish, often feeding on squid, mackerel, and tuna. Although marlin is considered the holy grail for sport anglers because of its enormous size and tremendous fight when hooked, marlin is also good eating.

Despite being caught commercially in Hawaii by long-line vessels and by trolling from smaller boats operating from Kona and Oahu, marlin is often an incidental catch in the long-line fishery, particularly when fishermen are targeting more commercially viable species offshore like tuna.

The meat of the marlin ranges from white to pink, although it varies somewhat from fish to fish. Marlin sold through the Honolulu fish auction tend to weigh between 80 and 300 pounds. The texture of marlin is firm with a mildly

"PANZANELLA SALAD"

4–6 slices (1-inch-thick) French baguette

Confit Garlic Shallot Oil
 (page 151), as needed

1 cup grilled asparagus, cut into 1-inch chunks

½ cup ramp leaves and bulbs, coated with oil and char-grilled

1 cup char-grilled roasted cherry tomatoes

2 tablespoons chives, cut into matchstick-lengths

6 large basil leaves, torn

Fresh squeezed lemon juice, as needed

Coarse sea salt, as needed

MARLIN

2 quarts water

4 ounces kosher salt

3 ounces granulated sugar

½ Meyer lemon, sliced

½ orange, sliced

½ grapefruit, sliced

2½ pounds marlin fillets or steaks

Olive oil, as needed

Continued on page 22

pronounced flavor. Because marlin is an excellent source of healthy, extra-lean protein, and is low in saturated fats and sodium, it's appearing in fish markets and on menus more frequently. It's also worth noting that marlin landed by trollers is usually larger, whereas the long-line marlin tends to have a higher fat content from the deeper waters in which it inhabits.

To make the "Panzanella Salad":

Dress the bread liberally with the Confit Garlic Shallot Oil, brushing well onto each side. Toast the bread on the grill over medium-hot coals or underneath the broiler. Toast should be well-charred but not excessively crispy or dry. Set aside.

In a medium-size mixing bowl, add the grilled asparagus, ramp leaves and bulbs, roasted cherry tomatoes, chives, and basil. Toss with fresh lemon juice and a little of the Confit Garlic Shallot Oil. Season to taste with coarse sea salt.

To make the Marlin:

In a small saucepot over medium heat, add the water, salt, sugar, and the lemon, orange, and grapefruit slices. Heat the mixture just until the salt and sugar have fully dissolved. Allow to cool completely. Once cooled, cover the marlin and allow to sit in the refrigerator for at least 1 hour, ideally for 2½ hours. Remove the marlin from the brine. Dry thoroughly with paper towels to remove any excess moisture and coat lightly with olive oil.

Grill the marlin steaks over intensely high heat using natural hardwood lump charcoal, cooking the fish on both sides until the flesh is well marked and the internal temperature is at least 165°F (for tips on grilling, see page xxxi).

To Serve: Arrange the toast onto a serving dish. Spoon a liberal amount of the "Panzanella Salad" over the toast. Place a portion of the grilled marlin next to the salad and finish with another spoonful of the salad.

SUGGESTED PAIRING

Muscadet-Sèvre et Maine "Sur Lie," Loire Valley, France

A lesser-known wine style hails from the heavily maritime-influenced Western Loire Valley. Made from the Melon de Bourgogne grape, this wine undergoes a traditional wine-making technique, Sur Lie, that helps impart flavor and texture. Its gentle creaminess stands up to grilled seafood, but its acid matches well with a fresh herbaceous salad.

OPAH CRUDO

SERVES 8-12

ALTERNATIVE FISH: HADDOCK, MAHI-MAHI, TUNA

This submission from Roast colleague Bradley Ball utilizes the prize cut of the opah for an incredibly simple and unique experience that makes perfect use of your available time when sunshine is in abundance. Honestly, this dish screams summertime. The goal of this recipe is to create something fresh and quick. No one wins if you miss out on a perfect day outdoors to slave away in the kitchen the entire time. If you're unfamiliar with how to slice the opah sashimi style, go online or seek out a local resource to help you. You can also have your fishmonger slice it for you.

Opah

Opah, or moonfish, is one of the most colorful of the commercial fish species available in California and Hawaii. A silvery-gray upper body color shades to a rose red dotted with white spots toward the belly. Its fins are crimson, and its large eyes are encircled with gold. The moonfish's unique round yet narrow profile may be the origin of its name.

The opah was viewed as a good luck fish by old-time long-line fishermen, who would give it away as a gesture of goodwill rather than sell it. Only recently has this species become commercially important. Opah are not found in schools, and thus are not caught in any quantity. They are a wandering pelagic species, often found in the company of tunas and billfish. Individual fish are regularly hooked incidentally by long-line boats fishing over seamounts. Landings follow no set pattern in any area, but the presence of opah at the depths of long-line fishing gear may be related to vertical migrations from the deep in search of food. Virtually all opah landed by long-liners is sold fresh through the Honolulu fish auction. Opah landed in Hawaii range from 60 to over 200 pounds. The entire opah catch is marketed as whole, fresh fish. Most are filleted for restaurant use, both in Hawaii and for export to the US mainland.

PICKLED FRESNO CHILIES

1 cup apple cider vinegar

1 cup distilled white vinegar

2 cups water

4 teaspoons salt

8 garlic cloves, smashed and peeled

8 allspice berries

16 fresh laurel leaves, or 4 dried bay leaves

1 pound Fresno chilies

OPAH CRUDO

1 pound opah top loin, sliced sashimi style

1 grapefruit, peeled and cut into segments, see below

2 whole Pickled Fresno Chilies, shaved paper-thin

Flake salt, as needed

Italian extra-virgin olive oil, as needed

Cilantro leaves, to garnish

TO MAKE THE PICKLED FRESNO CHILIES:

In a non reactive pot over medium-high heat, add both vinegars, water, salt, garlic, allspice, and laurel leaves. Bring to a boil. Remove from heat and allow to cool for 15 minutes. Pack the chilies into a sterilized container and cover well with the brine. Seal and allow to sit for at least 1 week.

HOW TO SEGMENT A GRAPEFRUIT

Place the grapefruit onto a cutting board, and using a very sharp utility knife, slice the ends from the fruit at the stem and perfectly parallel to the first cut. The goal is to imagine a perfect vertical line from the center of the fruit upon removing each end. Once firmly placed onto your cutting board, carve the skin of the fruit, making arcs with your knife cuts, starting at the top of the fruit and meeting at the bottom of the grapefruit. The cut should reveal the interior flesh of the grapefruit. Move your knife to remove the next portion of the peel, using the arc presented by the previous cut as a guide. "Peel" the remaining skin of the fruit and trim up any spots of pith that remain.

Continued on page 28

Hold the fruit firmly using a towel (to provide a better grip, and to protect your hand) and use a small, sharp knife to cut on one side of the skin that defines a segment of fruit. Make an additional cut on the opposite side of the first cut to release the segment of fruit. The remaining portion of fruit should be free of any skin. Reserve the segments in a small dish, and squeeze any remaining juice from the "skeleton" of grapefruit to cover.

To make the Opah Crudo:

Arrange the slices of opah onto a serving platter. Garnish the slices of fish with the grapefruit segments and shaved slices of the Pickled Fresno Chilies. Top the fish with flake salt. Finish with a light drizzle of the olive oil and a small spoonful of remaining grapefruit juice. Garnish with the cilantro leaves.

NOTE: There is no substitute for a high-end finishing olive oil. Do a little research before making a purchase, as there are many imposters to wade through. Keep a bottle hidden and use for simple finishing touches such as this. Look for a DOP label on whatever you purchase, signifying the authenticity of the olive oil.

SUGGESTED PAIRING

Gewürztraminer, Pfalz, Germany

When fully developed, this wine provides an unparalleled sipping experience. Textbook flavors of lychee, pepper spice, and sweet fruit harmoniously dance with mouth-filling acidity. Odd to this part of Germany, Gewürztraminer finds its balance in the dry and sunny areas sitting atop high elevation vineyards. Look for a style that provides enough acid to balance the sweetness and cut through any spiciness this dish might provide.

SCALLOP AGUACHILE

This ceviche-style recipe is the result of a special request made to prepare a refreshing and light alternative to the heavier flavors often found on our menu during the heart of winter in Michigan. The dish is a welcome reminder of warmer weather, and it instantly found a permanent home in our first course offerings. You can also assemble onto a platter for entertaining a large group.

The origins of this recipe preparation specify a very brief marinade of the seafood just prior to serving as opposed to the longer marinade commonly found in traditional ceviches. In other words, have all the ingredients and preparations completed before introducing the acidic lime juice to the sea scallops. Excessive exposure to the acid will cause the scallops to become tough and rubbery. Of course, use only the freshest and highest-quality sea scallops available, which are typically dry-packed. The U-10 in reference to the scallops below means there are ten or fewer to the pound, so they are quite large and you only need a few to make a meal.

Sea Scallops

The sea scallop, with its a brightly-colored, symmetrical, fan-shaped shell, is a favorite among seafood lovers. Although scallops inhabit all the world's oceans, most sea scallops served in the United States come from the Canadian and Atlantic waters.

Believe it or not, sea scallops can be considered bycatch. In this instance, they are collected by commercial fishermen using a bottom trawl for other ground species, particularly in the Canadian and British Columbia regions, or by dredging, a common fishing method in the Canadian Atlantic and US Mid-Atlantic in which large, wire-mesh bags are dragged along the seafloor by inshore and offshore trawlers targeting cod or skate.

Like oysters, scallops have a single central adductor muscle, and the larger it is, the more expensive the scallop. How sea scallops are packed also contributes to price.

Whipped Avocado

2 ripe avocados

1½ teaspoons white wine vinegar

2 tablespoons olive oil

Sea salt, to taste

Aquachile Sauce

1 jalapeño pepper, stem removed

2 garlic cloves, peeled

2 cups chopped cucumber

¼ cup flat-leaf parsley

⅛ cup mint leaves

¼ cup cilantro leaves

Scallops

6 large (U-10) dry-packed fresh sea scallops

⅓ cup freshly squeezed lime juice

To Make the Whipped Avocado:

Halve the avocados, remove the pit, and scoop the flesh into the bowl of a food processor or blender. Blend the avocado, and while the blender is processing, slowly add the vinegar and then oil in a thin stream. Stop to scrape down the sides of the bowl, and season with salt to taste. This can also be made by hand in a mixing bowl by simply mashing the avocado well with a fork or potato masher, then whisking in the vinegar and oil until homogenous.

Note: If preparing this recipe in advance, it will be important to correctly store the final product to reduce the occurrence of oxidization, or browning. To do so, tightly pack the avocado mixture to eliminate any air bubbles, then pack tightly in a sealed container to reduce the amount of exposed air.

Continued on page 33

The higher-quality sea scallops are typically referred to as dry-packed sea scallops, meaning they have not been treated with phosphates, as opposed to wet-packing, in which the scallop is first bathed in phosphates for adding water weight. Such scallops are often tougher and less flavorful than their dry counterparts. You're also not paying for added water when purchasing dry-packed sea scallops.

To make the Aquachile Sauce:

In a blender, add the jalapeño, garlic, cucumber, parsley, mint, and cilantro leaves. Purée until smooth, then strain to remove any pulp. Set aside until ready to use.

Note: In the restaurant, we use a cold-process thickening agent derived from modified tapioca starch called UltraTex 8. This helps to thicken the sauce for presentation purposes when plating. UltraTex 8 is available from high-end spice merchants or available online.

To make the Scallops:

Slice the scallops into coins ¼-inch thick. Lay the slices of scallop into a non reactive dish and toss well with the lime juice. Marinate for 3 to 4 minutes just before serving.

To Serve: Spoon a liberal amount of the Aquachile Sauce onto a plate and place 3 or 4 slices of the marinated scallops around the dish. Spoon or pipe the whipped avocado on and around the scallop, finishing the plate with a fresh squeeze of lime juice, some coarse flake salt, and garnish with a few fresh leaves of cilantro.

Optional Garnish: The dish lends itself well to the addition of Sweet Pickled Pearl Onions (page 173).

Suggested Pairing

Txakolina, Basque, Spain

This odd and hard to pronounce wine is crisp, acidic, and almost bubbly. Hints of citrus, melon, and salty notes play effortlessly with the touch of effervesce. It's at home in the Basque region of Northern Spain, and although foreign to most palates, it is the favorite pour in the culinary mecca of San Sebastian. Enjoyed primarily with raw and lightly marinated styles of preparation, it's a must for a hot summer day.

RED ROCK CRAB SALAD

SERVES 4

ALTERNATIVE FISH: BLUE CRAB, DUNGENESS CRAB, HIGH-QUALITY LUMP CRABMEAT

This incredibly simple and refreshing crab salad immediately transports me to every picnic table of each campground we visited as a child while my mother would serve a version of this salad on days that it was "too hot to cook." The dish is thoroughly reinforced with complex flavors resulting from the foundational recipes, with pure magic delivered via the dill pollen. Dill pollen is available from high-end spice retailers, and a little goes a long way. We actively crush the pollen between our fingers when adding it to a recipe. At the restaurant, we serve this salad with what we refer to as Spicy Greens. Local organic farmer and vegetable magician Charles Johnson raises a mesclun mix of lettuces that are so hearty and intense with the addition of mustard and horseradish greens that you are physically moved by their consumption. A substitution of peppery arugula or watercress would be appropriate here, unless you know CJ, in which case, use what he offers.

For more information on red rock crab, see page 9.

½ cup Garlic Shallot Mayonnaise (page 163)

1 tablespoon fresh minced dill

½ tablespoon minced shallot

2 pounds fresh rock crabmeat

¾ cup Salt Cured Celery (page 108), small dice

1 teaspoon fresh lemon juice

¼ teaspoon dill pollen

1 large bunch spicy greens

Confit Garlic Shallot Oil (page 151) or olive oil, as needed

6 medium-size boiled eggs, sliced into wedges

2 stalks celery, shaved

In a small mixing bowl, combine the Garlic Shallot Mayonnaise with dill and shallot. Set aside.

Place the crabmeat into a medium-size mixing bowl, and add the Salt Cured Celery. Gently fold in the mayonnaise mixture and lemon juice, careful not to break down the crab too much, preserving its texture. Sprinkle in the dill pollen as a final step, rubbing between your fingers as you incorporate.

TO SERVE: Dress the spicy greens with a bit of Confit Garlic Shallot Oil or olive oil, and place onto separate plates or a large serving platter. Top with the crab salad, and garnish with wedges of the boiled eggs and a bit of fresh, crisp, shaved celery.

SUGGESTED PAIRING

Albariño, Rias Baixas, Spain

Rias Baixas sits in the northwestern corner of Spain, bordering the Atlantic Ocean. It boasts a unique type of viticulture where vines are trained to grow up stone pergolas that allow the rich maritime breeze to flow through and provide maximum circulation, ultimately allowing the grapes to fully ripen. Dominating the landscape is a grape called Albariño. Styles can vary from area to area but most are crisp, dry, and elegant with flavors ranging from fresh stone fruits to pineapple and mango.

OLIVE OIL POACHED SKIPJACK TUNA & GREEN BEAN "NIÇOISE" SALAD

SERVES 4

ALTERNATIVE FISH: ALBACORE, MAHI-MAHI, WAHOO

There are many strong opinions regarding the elements necessary to categorize a "Niçoise." Paul Bocuse will have to forgive us for the inclusion of tuna. The remaining ingredients are either historically celebrated or presented simply because they're delicious. Call it what you like—this salad is an incredible celebration of the midsummer harvest. Summertime green beans, incidentally, inspired the research that yielded surprising and controversial results.

SKIPJACK TUNA

There are roughly fifteen species of tuna recognized worldwide. The Skipjack, considered a medium-size tuna in the tuna family, is also known as the stripped tuna and can be found in tropical and warm-temperate waters around the globe.

Many home cooks may not be familiar with the Skipjack tuna, but they're probably familiar with the end product. That's because more than 70 percent of the American canned tuna market comes from Skipjack. It's often labeled as Chunk Light Tuna.

Because Skipjack is the most abundant species of tuna, they do end up in a lot of fishermen's nets. Even though Skipjack is the most widely fished of the tuna species, it can be considered bycatch when landed by commercial fishermen who use large purse-seine nets to target other tuna species, such as yellowfin, albacore, bigeye, and the large Bluefin tuna.

Skipjack tuna, other than the canned variety, is sold fresh and frozen, as well as dried, salted, and smoked. It's very popular in Japanese cuisine, in which it's consumed raw as well as smoked. Unlike some of the larger tunas like the Bluefin, Skipjack is known for fewer amounts of mercury contamination.

OLIVE OIL POACHED SKIPJACK TUNA

Olive oil, as needed

6 garlic cloves, smashed and peeled

3 fresh laurel leaves (or 1 medium bay leaf)

12 whole black peppercorns, toasted

1 lemon peel, cut in strips

1½ pounds skipjack tuna fillet

2 or 3 tablespoons Caper Anchovy Vinaigrette (page 145)

½ cup fresh chévre (from your local cheese maker)

VINEGAR POACHED POTATOES

¾ pound small waxy potatoes (new potatoes or French fingerlings)

4 cups white distilled vinegar

2 sprigs fresh thyme

1 tablespoon dill seed

1 tablespoon celery seed

CHILLED GREEN BEANS

2 pounds chilled green beans, ends trimmed (see page 39 for The Green Blanching Method)

Dill Vinaigrette (page 155), as needed

2 tablespoons marcona almonds

TO MAKE THE OLIVE OIL POACHED SKIPJACK TUNA:

In a heavy-bottomed saucepot, add enough olive oil to bring the cooking level up to 2 inches. Add the garlic, laurel leaves (or bay leaf), peppercorns, and strips of lemon peel. Gently bring the oil to a simmer (165°F) and add the fish. Once the oil has come back up to temperature, cook the tuna until well done (145°F). Remove from heat and allow the fish and oil to cool. Place in the refrigerator and reserve until ready to use. Note: The flavored olive oil can also be strained and held in the refrigerator for future use.

ALTERNATIVE METHOD FOR SOUS VIDE COOKS:

Place the tuna fillet into a large vacuum bag. Add the garlic, laurel leaves (or bay leaf), peppercorns, and strips of lemon peel. Add 1¼ cups olive oil to the bag and vacuum seal. Place the bag in a thermal immersion circulator bath (set to 120°F) and allow to cook for 27 minutes. Place the bag into an ice bath and allow to cool.

Continued on page 38

To make the Vinegar Poached Potatoes:

In a saucepot over medium-high heat, add the potatoes, vinegar, thyme, dill seed, and celery seed. Bring to a boil, reduce to a simmer, and cook until the potatoes are fork tender. Remove from heat and chill until ready to use.

To Serve: Flake the chilled tuna into large chunks and place into a medium-size mixing bowl. Toss well to coat with the Caper Anchovy Vinaigrette. Place the Chilled Green Beans into a large mixing bowl and dress thoroughly with the Dill Vinaigrette. Pile the beans onto a large, chilled platter, and scatter the Vinegar Poached Potatoes throughout in a pleasant random manner. Pinch the fresh chévre over the beans and finish with the marcona almonds, scattering around the plate. Place the tuna at the center of the beans and serve.

SUGGESTED PAIRING

Rosé, Costières de Nimes, France

The Southern Rhone wine region is a coastal region off the Mediterranean that is covered in round sedimentary rocks that get hot during the day and radiate to the nearby vines during the cool nights. This relationship allows for elegance and purity that shine through even in its blush style of wine. Grenache, Syrah, and Mouvedre lend tart red strawberry fruit and plenty of weight to stand up to even the meatiest of fish.

THE GREEN BLANCHING METHOD

One of the most thoroughly stressed preparations in our restaurant, Green Blanching, requires vast amounts of both "cooking" mediums: an incredible amount of heavily salted water at a rip-roaring boil, and a large ice bath, responsible for stopping the cooking of the beans upon their arrival to the vibrant green state present when expertly executed.

Fill your largest pot 80 percent full of cold, fresh water and place over high heat. Season the water aggressively with salt (and we mean *aggressively*). Cover, and bring to a boil.

Prepare your ice bath by using a large bucket or tub (similar in volume to the cooking pot boiling the water) and prepare with equal parts ice to water. Reserve next to the cooking pot.

Depending on the size of your boil pot relative to the quantity of green beans, you may need to blanch the beans in batches. Never add more than 20 percent relative volume of beans to the water, as this will cause the temperature of the water to drop significantly. Upon adding the beans, the water should return to a boil within 15 to 20 seconds. If it takes significantly longer, add a smaller batch of beans for the next round. Allow the beans to cook in the boiling water for 60 to 90 seconds, or until their color turns vibrant green and retains a noticeable crunch. Remove the beans and immediately plunge into the ice bath, agitating the beans to cool them quickly. Repeat the process with the remaining beans. Note: If most ice in your bath is melting prior to all the beans being cooled, simply add a significant amount of ice and continue to proceed.

Remove the beans from the ice bath immediately once they've cooled to ensure they do not take on any moisture from the bath. Dry the beans well and reserve.

CHILLED POACHED TRIGGERFISH, SAVORY GRANOLA & GREEN SMOOTHIE BROTH

Serves 4
Alternative fish: crab, grouper, snapper

Amazing friend and personal trainer Gwadue Bossuah dominates West Michigan's fitness culture with his everlasting energy and positive attitude. We've come together for many business meetings, seeking perspective and a friendly ear, often before the sun has shown itself to the day. This preparation is an incredibly fun way to make fun of your trainer when he visits your restaurant and happens to bring his team of talented professionals from Fzique Grand Rapids for dinner. Juicing the ingredients for the broth is intended to preserve the flavors well experienced by anyone familiar with an early morning workout, and the resulting dish is a perfect way to prepare an incredible lunch for the following day's recovery.

Triggerfish

There are about forty species of triggerfish, often brightly colored, which inhabit the tropical and subtropical oceans, with the greatest species coming from the Indo-Pacific. With their radiant raylike fins and small mouths, triggerfish can be found foraging around reefs, wrecks, piers, and rocky outcrops, where they use their sharp teeth and strong jaws to crush shells, mussels, and other prey.

Despite these colorful reef fish's rather odd appearance and rough skin, some are quite flavorful. The gray (or grey) triggerfish, named after its uniformly gray coloration, is excellent table-fare, while other species like the triton triggerfish may be ciguatoxic and should be avoided.

The gray triggerfish, which may also go by the names leatherjacket or filefish, has small, flaky flesh with a slightly sweet and meaty flavor, making them sought after by recreational and some commercial fishermen, especially in the Southeast Atlantic off Florida and the US Gulf of Mexico. Because triggerfish are not typically targeted commercially for consumption, they are often the result of incidental catches by fisheries pursuing snapper and grouper.

Garnish
2 celery stalks, trimmed and leaves removed

4 tart green apples

2 teaspoons citric acid

Chilled Poached Triggerfish
4 quarts coconut water

1 tablespoon coriander seed, toasted

1 vanilla bean, split and scraped

1 head garlic, halved lengthwise

2 tablespoons Matcha Green Tea Powder (or 3 tablespoons high-quality green tea)

2 limes, halved

2 pounds triggerfish fillets, allowed to come up to room temperature for 30 minutes

Savory Granola
3 ounces coconut oil

2 ounces apple cider

1 ounce honey

1 teaspoon kosher salt

½ cup rolled oats

½ cup + 1 tablespoon pumpkin seeds

¼ cup black cumin seed (aka black onion seed or nigella seed)

5 tablespoons flaxseed

1 teaspoon coriander seed, toasted and ground

½ teaspoon anise seed, toasted and ground

Green Smoothie Broth
Makes 2 cups

2 cups kale leaves, chopped

1 cup spinach leaves, chopped

1 small carrot, chopped

1 stalk celery, chopped

2 sprigs fresh mint

3 sprigs flat-leaf parsley

1 apple, cored and cut into pieces

½ lime, peeled

½ cup fennel bulb, chopped

1 cup cucumber, chopped

Ultra-Tex 3, as needed

Continued on page 42

To make the Garnish:

Using a vegetable peeler, draw across each celery stalk to achieve long ribbons of celery. Place the shaved celery pieces into a small container and cover with cold water. Place into refrigerator until ready to serve. Next, peel and core two of the apples. Juice or purée the apples and strain. Stir in the citric acid immediately and set aside. Dice the remaining two apples into varied sizes ranging from ⅛ to ¼ inch. Place the apples into a ziptop bag along with the citric-apple liquid, removing as much air as possible. Allow the apples to marinate for at least 1 hour, ideally overnight.

To make the Chilled Poached Triggerfish:

In a heavy-bottomed saucepot, add the coconut water, coriander, vanilla, garlic, green tea, and limes. Bring to a boil. Remove from heat and let infuse for at least 30 minutes. Strain and return the liquid to the pot, discarding the solids. Bring the liquid to a simmer and add the triggerfish fillets. Cook the fish at this simmer until a digital-read thermometer registers 135°F, roughly 12 minutes. Remove from the heat and allow the fish to cool fully in the cooking liquid. Reserve in the refrigerator until ready to use.

To make the Savory Granola:

Preheat the oven to 325°F. Add the coconut oil to a small saucepot. Heat over medium. Remove from the heat, allow to cool slightly, and stir in the apple cider, honey, and kosher salt. In a medium-size mixing bowl, add the oats, pumpkin seeds, black cumin seed, flaxseed, coriander seed, and anise seed. Add the coconut oil mixture to the dry ingredients and mix well with a rubber spatula. Spread the mixture in an even layer on a parchment or tray lined with a nonstick baking mat and bake in the oven for about 30 minutes, or until slightly crunchy. Note: The granola will continue to harden as it cools.

To make the Green Smoothie Broth:

Using a home juicer, juice the kale, spinach, carrot, celery, mint, parsley, apple, lime, fennel, and cucumber. Note: When juicing leafy greens, it is helpful to push the harder vegetables through after, which help the greens go through. Alternatively, you may blend the ingredients together in a kitchen blender and then strain. Thicken the mixture slightly with Ultra-Tex 3, which will allow you to better present the delicate flavors in the juice without the need to heat and alter the taste.

Ultra-Tex 3 is a cold-or hot-process thickening agent derived from tapioca. It doesn't impart any flavor, is resistant to clumping, and will very likely change your life. The product is available through any high-end spice merchant or online.

To Serve: Place the chilled triggerfish onto the center of a cold, shallow bowl and top with a spoonful of Savory Granola. Garnish with the apples and shaved celery, and finish with ¼ cup of Green Smoothie Broth over the top.

SUGGESTED PAIRING

White Bordeaux Blend, Bordeaux, France

Bordeaux winemakers are well-versed in the art of blending, with each grape playing off the other to bring a unique characteristic to the wine. Sauvignon Blanc, Semillon, and Muscadelle make up most blends. White Bordeaux tends to be light and fruit-forward while exhibiting delicate aromas of grass and flowers, making for an ideal pairing with light and flaky fish.

SOUPS & STEWS

Midwestern Cobia & Red Rock Crab Boil   46

Haddock Chowder   49

Green Chile Lionfish, Triggerfish & Scallop Cioppino   52

Roasted Potato Cream with Smoked Mullet &
Crispy Fried Onion   56

Smoked Mullet   60

Red Rock Crab Bisque   62

Spanish Fisherman's Stew   64

MIDWESTERN COBIA & RED ROCK CRAB BOIL

SERVES 8–12

ALTERNATIVE FISH: SALMON, TUNA

Nothing says summer better than a table surrounded by friends and family, the sunshine filling the horizon as the day begins to acknowledge its nighttime counterpart, and a feast enjoyed with laughter and tales from the long day's adventures. In the restaurant, we cook this dish using separate cooking methods, assembling them for a quick dip in the broth before being piled onto newspaper or into large bowls. You're welcome to apply this philosophy to the ingredients listed below while utilizing the Alternative Cooking Method. Regardless of how you prepare it, this is a perfect dish for a group or scaled down for a small supper.

Cobia

According to National Geographic, cobia is the "Other Other White Meat."

Cobia, like bluefish, is the only member of its fish genus, making it truly unique. Because these large predators seldom congregate in groups, making them too difficult to harvest, they're not often targeted by commercial fishermen. Instead, cobia are usually caught recreationally or as bycatch by fishermen looking for other species.

Cobia are long, slim, and dark brown in color with a broad, flat head and single dorsal fin. They are occasionally seen following sharks and rays. This fish, which can reach a length of 6 feet and weigh more than 100 pounds, is found from Virginia to Florida and the Gulf of Mexico and often spotted around buoys, pilings, and wrecks.

With a firm white flesh, similar to that of Spanish mackerel, cobia is a delicious-tasting fish. Although cobia should be eaten fresh, their fillets freeze well and are suited to most cooking styles. Also be aware that cobia, like marlin, swordfish, and tuna, often contain high amount amounts of mercury (see mercury chart, page xxix).

6 quarts Fumet (page 157)

12 ounces butter

½ cup Old Bay Seasoning

1 (12-ounce) can Stroh's (or your favorite local craft brew pilsner)

4 sprigs fresh thyme

1 tablespoon red chili flakes

1 medium-sized sweet onion, peeled and shaved

1 bulb fennel, shaved

4 fresh laurel leaves (or 1 bay leaf)

3 whole Caramelized Lemons (page 130), reserving some slices for garnish

3 pounds small, low-starch potatoes (fingerling or German butterball)

4 ears local organic sweet corn, cut into thirds

2 pounds well-sourced pork sausage, cut into 2-inch pieces

3 pounds cobia, cleaned and cut into 2-inch chunks

2 pounds cooked red rock crabmeat and claws

Spicy Garlic Butter (page 172), for garnish

Flat-leaf parsley, chopped, for garnish

In a 10- or 12-quart stockpot (ideally one that will accept a basket or insert like a pasta pot and strainer), add the Fumet, butter, Old Bay Seasoning, beer, thyme, chili flakes, onion, fennel, laurel leaves (or bay leaf), and the lemons. Note: The broth can also be made using a clean turkey fryer/basket and cooked outdoors over a propane burner. Bring the broth to a boil, hold the temperature, and add some water if left unattended too long and the liquid reduces.

Add the potatoes to the boiling liquid and allow to cook for 12 minutes. Add the corn and pork sausage, and cook for 3 or 4 minutes. Add the cobia and allow to cook for 2 minutes. Add the crab and immediately remove the pot from the heat and let sit for 2 minutes undisturbed. Gently pull the basket from the broth, or gently scoop out the contents using a wire strainer.

Continued on page 48

To Serve: Place the potatoes, corn, pork sausage, cobia, and crab onto platters, a newspaper-lined picnic table, or large bowls, ensuring an even distribution of each ingredient. Finish with a good ladle or two of the broth (stir well first) over the top. Garnish with the Spicy Garlic Butter, parsley, and the additional caramelized lemons.

Alternative Cooking Method:

- Prepare the broth and potatoes as described above.
- Coat the sweet corn with some Spicy Garlic Butter (page 172) before grilling over blistering hot coals for an incredible visual garnish (for tips on grilling, see page xxxi).
- Confit the sausage, using the same method as the Confit Pork Belly (page 152). Cook to an internal temperature of 140°F and finish on the grill for a nice char.
- Prepare the cobia using the Butter-Poach method described on page 7.
- Add the broth just to finish and reheat prior to serving.

Suggested Pairing

Champagne, Champagne, France

The Champagne region of France sits just northeast of Paris. Its proximity to the grand city has allowed for the adoration of royalty and nobility throughout its rich history. The beauty of its cuvée is born from a specific process during production. Laws deem specific vineyard practices as well as certain grape-pressing techniques region to region and, most importantly, a secondary fermentation of the wine in the bottle to create its famous bubble. Styles can span from concentrated to creamy and pair well with all seafood or just as a standalone aperitif.

HADDOCK CHOWDER

SERVES 6

ALTERNATIVE FISH: HALIBUT, MONKFISH, ALASKAN BLACK COD/SABLEFISH, AMBERJACK, SEA BASS

This incredibly simple chowder is a thorough celebration of the East Coast, and while perfectly enjoyable in every season, it couldn't be more appropriate on a cold, early fall day. The leaves barely begin to turn color in the Midwest, and I'm more than ready to prepare a big pot for the staff at the restaurant. Spend a Sunday morning preparing the Fumet and the additional Foundational Recipes, and your Sunday afternoon will never be the same.

HADDOCK

Haddock, not to be confused with pollock, is a deep water fish often found in the cold waters of the North Atlantic Ocean, particularly the Gulf of Maine and Georges Bank. They average 2 to 6 pounds in weight.

Haddock, although fished for year-round by commercial fishermen, can be considered bycatch when they are caught in the same seine nets as their relative and a heavily targeted species, the Atlantic cod. Haddock are also landed by trawlers and long-line fishermen. Once overfished, Atlantic haddock is now almost fully recovered off the East Coast.

Haddock is sold year-round, both fresh and frozen. The most sustainable Haddock to purchase fresh are those caught by long-line or bottom trawls. The meat, which should feel firm to the touch, is lean and white, which becomes whiter when cooked.

HADDOCK

12–14 pieces (2 to 3 ounces each), haddock, cleaned and trimmed

Kosher salt, as needed

Granulated sugar, as needed

Cooking oil (e.g., vegetable, avocado, grapeseed)

CHOWDER

5 tablespoons rendered bacon fat

3 tablespoons salted butter

Slow Confit Fingerling Potatoes (page 151)

1½ cups Confit Pork Belly (page 152), diced into ½-inch cubes (or ¾ cup crispy cooked bacon)

1 cup Charred Leeks (page 149)

½ fresh fennel bulb, sliced very thin

2 tablespoons fresh shallot, peeled and minced

1 tablespoon fresh garlic, peeled and minced

3 sprigs fresh thyme

½ cup dry, crisp white wine

1 cup Caramelized Leeks (page 145)

1½ cups heavy cream

3 cups Fumet (page 157)

¼ cup fresh chives, minced

TO MAKE THE HADDOCK:

Pat the fish dry with a kitchen towel or paper towels. Season the fillets (thoroughly but not excessively) with a 50/50 mixture of the kosher salt and granulated sugar. Set the fillets into an appropriately sized dish and place in refrigerator for at least 2 hours.

Remove the fish from the refrigerator 30 minutes prior to cooking to allow the fish to come up in temperature. This will provide for even cooking of the fillet. Pat the fish dry using a kitchen towel or paper towel. Excess moisture on the fish will cause it to stick to the pan and may cause the fish to steam instead of sear.

Heat a large, heavy-bottomed sauté pan over medium heat until hot, about 3 to 4 minutes. Add enough cooking oil to just coat the bottom of the pan. Heat the oil for about 30 seconds before adding the fish. Place the fillets in the pan, laying the fish away from you and taking extreme care. Cook the fish until the bottom is golden brown and the fish releases easily from the pan, about 1 or 2 minutes.

Continued on page 50

If the fish seems to stick, it may need a short time longer. Carefully slide a fish spatula under the fish and flip to cook the remaining side. Remove from the heat when the color has turned throughout, and the flesh feels firm across the entire piece. Remove the fish and sprinkle with some more kosher salt after placing onto a paper towel–lined plate.

To make the Chowder:

Place a large Dutch oven over medium heat. Add the bacon fat and butter. Once the fats have melted and heated, add the Fingerling Potatoes and pork belly (or bacon). Allow the potatoes to sear in the pot until golden brown and they have developed a slight crust, about roughly 1 or 2 minutes. Add the Charred Leeks and sliced fennel, followed by the shallots. Cook for 10 to 15 seconds, giving the contents in the pot two or three stirs. Add the garlic, fresh thyme, and white wine. Do not allow the garlic to burn or take on any color. Let the wine reduce for 30 to 45 seconds, or until reduced by half. Add the Caramelized Leeks, cream, and Fumet. Bring the pot to a boil, and let the chowder reduce, cooking for 10 to 12 minutes, or until the liquid has reduced by about 70 percent. The remaining liquid should be thick and viscous, hearty enough to coat the back of a spoon. Remove the thyme sprigs.

To Serve: Distribute the chowder into six shallow bowls, ensuring an adequate distribution of the potatoes, pork, and vegetables. Place 2 or 3 pieces of seared haddock into each bowl. Garnish each portion with minced chives.

SUGGESTED PAIRING

English Pale Ale, London, England

Chowder and beer is a traditional combination in the northeast part of the United States. An English pale carries more malt than its American counterpart and therefore less bitterness. Caramel malt sweetness touched with flavors of apple and apricot will brighten up the rich cream base of any New England–style chowder.

GREEN CHILE LIONFISH, TRIGGERFISH & SCALLOP CIOPPINO

SERVES 4

ALTERNATIVE FISH: FLOUNDER, GROUPER, SNAPPER

This delightfully intense stew is a fun twist on the classic San Francisco dish. We feature the following recipe on the inaugural fall menu at our Kalamazoo restaurant. Principle Food & Drink. General manager and business partner Casey Longton would recommend a few cups of milk to accompany the tinge of heat delivered via the hatch chilies. For another level of complexity, smoke the chilies before roasting as we do in Fennville as an initial step to preserving a garden full of bumper crop chilies. Smoked or not, you'll dream of this version for weeks.

LIONFISH

If you're not familiar, lionfish, which are native to the reefs and rocky crevices of the Indo-Pacific, are an invasive species in the Atlantic Ocean that continues to threaten the native fish and the environment in the US Atlantic coastal waters. Experts believe people have been dumping unwanted lionfish from home aquariums into the Atlantic for the past twenty-five years.

Despite their relatively small size— about one foot—lionfish have very few enemies. They are aggressive carnivores that feed on primarily anything that can fit into their large, gaping mouths, including small commercially viable species such as snapper and grouper. Lionfish also have brightly-colored stripes and venomous needle like dorsal fins, making them undesirable prey for larger predators like sharks.

For humans, however, eating lionfish is good—and delicious. Not only are lionfish safe to eat (there is no venom in the flesh; only the spines contain venom, which would not cause poisoning if ingested), removing lionfish and consuming them as a seafood selection helps our reefs and native fish stocks recover from environmental pressures and lionfish predation. Lionfish is also a healthier choice than many other fish because studies have been shown they tend to be higher in heart-healthy omega-3

CIOPPINO BROTH

¼ cup olive oil

1 large sweet onion, peeled and small dice

12 cloves garlic, smashed and peeled

1 shallot, peeled and small dice

1 medium-size leek, dark green parts removed, halved and sliced

2 stalks celery, small dice

4 roasted green New Mexico or hatch chilies, seeds and stems removed, chopped

1 tablespoon fennel seed, toasted

¼ teaspoon red chili flakes

½ cup dry white wine

2 fresh laurel leaves (or 1 bay leaf)

3 pounds tomatillos, husked and halved

2 cups Fumet (page 157)

1 sprig fresh oregano

1 sprig fresh thyme

FRESH FISH

½ pound lionfish fillets

½ pound triggerfish fillets

6 large (U-10) sea scallops

Kosher salt, as needed

Granulated sugar, as needed

Olive oil, as needed

Butter, as needed

Flake salt, as needed

Pickled Green Tomatoes (page 167), for garnish

Garlic Bread (page 160)

TO MAKE THE CIOPPINO BROTH:

Heat a large stockpot over medium heat. Add the olive oil. Add the onion, garlic, shallot, leek, and celery, and cook until softened. Add the chilies, fennel, and chili flakes. Cook until fragrant. Add the wine and reduce by half. Add the laurel leaves, tomatillos, Fumet, oregano, and thyme. Bring to a boil, then lower to a simmer and reduce by 30 percent. Strain the broth and reserve.

TO MAKE THE FRESH FISH:

Season the lionfish, triggerfish, and scallops well with a 50/50 mixture of kosher salt and granulated sugar. Allow the seafood to sit at room temperature for 30 minutes. Transfer to paper towels and dry each piece of seafood.

fatty acids and lower in saturated fats and heavy metals such as mercury. Lionfish flesh is white, flaky, and firm, with a flavor similar to grouper or mahi-mahi. Today, more and more restaurants are adding lionfish to their menu.

For more information on triggerfish, see page 40.

PAN SIZE

It is imperative you use an adequately large sauté pan when searing fish at high heat or cooking fish in batches. You must provide an adequate amount of space between the individual pieces to ensure a consistent temperature of the pan. Each addition of fish will, in effect, cool the pan and lower the temperature of the sauté pan as it responds to the cooler temperature of the fish. Overcrowding the pan will cause the temperature to drop excessively and result in the fish sticking and subsequently steaming instead of searing.

Heat a large heavy-bottomed sauté pan over medium heat until hot, about 3 or 4 minutes. Add enough oil to just coat the bottom of the sauté pan. Heat the oil for 15 to 30 seconds, then add the lionfish fillets. Cook the fish until the bottom is golden-brown and the fish releases easily from the pan, about 1 or 2 minutes. If the fish seems to stick, it may need a short time longer. Carefully turn the fish over using a fish spatula and cook the other side. Add the butter into the sauté pan and allow the butter to melt. As the fish cooks on the second side, use a large metal spoon and tilt the pan to allow for the butter to collect on one side. Spoon the hot butter and baste the fish. Continue this basting throughout the remaining cooking time. Allow for caramelization of the fish and remove from heat when color has turned opaque throughout, and the flesh feels firm across the entire piece. Remove from the pan and sprinkle with coarse flake salt after placing onto paper towels to rest. Continue the same process with the triggerfish and sea scallops.

TO SERVE: Place a heaping ladle of the Cioppino Broth into a large serving bowl. Add the seafood throughout, and garnish with diced Pickled Green Tomatoes. Serve with some Garlic Bread, which is simply your vehicle for consuming the spicy and hearty broth.

SUGGESTED PAIRING

Zinfandel, Paso Robles, California

Reds from this region of the world can be potent but delicate. Fruit-forward flavors integrate with soft tannins to create an ideal pairing with a tomato-based fish stew. Tannin is created by grape skin and provides structure and astringency to a wine. Red wines can be a tough pair with seafood, but tomato-based stews provide a great opportunity.

ROASTED POTATO CREAM WITH SMOKED MULLET & CRISPY FRIED ONION

SERVES 6-8

ALTERNATIVE FISH: SMOKED SALMON, OR OTHER SMOKED FISH

During one of our weekly menu meetings, my culinary team developed the idea of roasting potato skins and adding them into a broth after exploring the opportunity to deconstruct and reimagine the classic appetizer. The roasted potato skins in this recipe add a surprising depth of flavor to the richness of the potato cream, while the Crispy Fried Onions are not only addictive (be careful—they actually need to make it to the dinner table), but also the perfect addition to, well . . . everything. For some extra deliciousness, replace the cornstarch mixture with the Country Dredge (page 153), or if feeling truly adventurous, use the Sweet Pickled Pearl Onions (page 173) along with the Country Dredge, and garnish with pan-fried slices of Confit Pork Belly (page 152). It's absolutely magical. As for the Smoked Mullet, it's added to this dish as a featured garnish. Similar to smoked salmon, smoked mullet can be purchased online or at select seafood markets either as cold-smoked or hot-smoked. I included a recipe at the end if you're feeling adventurous and would like to try smoking mullet yourself.

MULLET

Mullet is an abundant coastal fish, particularly in the Gulf of Mexico and the Caribbean where the species thrives in the tropical and warm temperate waters. They're also abundant along the east coast of the United States, southern parts of the west coast, and throughout other tropical regions of the world. They're often known for leaping out of the water in large schools.

Mullet caught in the Gulf of Mexico are either silver mullet or the larger striped mullet. Because mullet are vegetarian, they are rarely taken by rod and reel and are considered easy bycatch for fishermen using nets to catch other more desirable species.

Because mullet are rather fatty and oily, like mackerel, it is best eaten when smoked. Having been served as an important food source in the Mediterranean during Roman times, mullet are easy to clean and usually smoked "butterfly" style.

ROASTED POTATO CREAM

4 medium-size russet potatoes

Olive oil, as needed

Kosher salt, as needed

¼ cup salted butter

1 medium-size sweet onion, peeled and diced

3 garlic cloves, peeled

4 cups Fumet (page 157)

2 cups whole milk

1½ cups cream

½ cup sour cream

Sea salt, to taste

Smoked mullet, as garnish

Fresh chives, minced, as garnish

CRISPY FRIED ONION

1 large sweet onion

2 cups cornstarch

2 teaspoons finely ground black pepper

Cooking oil, as needed

Fine salt, to taste

TO MAKE THE ROASTED POTATO CREAM:

Preheat the oven to 375°F.

Fill a tall container with cold water. Peel the russet potatoes and transfer to the cold water, reserving all the potato peelings in a separate container that has also been filled with a moderate amount of cold water. Note: Reserving the potatoes and peelings in cold water reduces any oxidization (browning) of the potatoes during preparation. Next, dice the peeled potatoes to a medium, uniform size and return to the water. Set aside.

Rinse the potato peelings by pouring out the water from the container and cover again with cold water. Repeat this process until the water being drained is clear.

Continued on page 58

Place the potato peelings onto a baking sheet, drizzle with olive oil, and season lightly with kosher salt. Roast the peels in the oven for 10 to 12 minutes, or until caramelized and slightly crispy.

Next, place a large Dutch oven or soup pot over medium heat. Melt the butter, and sauté the onion for 3 or 4 minutes until it softens and just begins to take on color. Add the garlic and cook for an additional 1 or 2 minutes (do not burn the garlic!). Add the roasted potato peels, Fumet, milk, cream, and the diced potatoes (drained well). Slowly heat the mixture until it reaches a gentle simmer, and cook for 25 to 30 minutes, or until potatoes are tender. Remove from heat.

Blend the contents from the pot using an immersion blender, or transfer in small batches to a kitchen blender. Note: If mixture is hot and you're using a kitchen blender, be very careful and only fill the jar halfway. Stir in the sour cream until blended. Season to taste with sea salt.

To make the Crispy Fried Onion:

Shave the onion (use a Japanese mandolin or a steady hand) to ⅛-inch thickness. Place the cornstarch and black pepper in a shallow dish and add the shaved onion, separating the rings as you go. Thoroughly coat the onion with the cornstarch mixture, allowing the onion to rest in the mixture for 1 or 2 minutes before removing from the dish and eliminating any excess cornstarch. Deep-fry or panfry the onion until golden brown and crispy. Remove from the oil and transfer to a plate lined with paper towels. Season with some fine salt. Note: The

onion will benefit from being fried at a lower temperature than what is typically recommended for frying (we suggest 315°F to 325°F). Too high of a frying temperature will cause the onion to become excessively dark and subsequently bitter.

TO SERVE: Portion the soup into serving bowls and garnish with the Crispy Fried Onion, smoked mullet, and fresh minced chives.

SUGGESTED PAIRING

Soave, Veneto, Italy

Soave, a region, not a grape, was once the most popular Italian wine in the United States. These northeastern Italian wines deliver incredible intensity and structure. The nearby Po Valley produces mists that carry over the vineyards and irrigate as well as bring viticulture hazards. The thick skin that protects it and gives it the ability to ripen later in the season creates distinct flavors of bitter almond, lemon, and stone. Soave is a wonderful food wine and can find a partner in most seafood.

SMOKED MULLET

For the first two years of operation, I could achieve all the smoking needs of the restaurant (sizable, ranging from 50 to 400 pounds per week) on a small, backyard-style barbecue smoker. Eventually, we had the ability to purchase a larger unit, welded by hand by a gentleman in Virginia and towed to Michigan behind an old, weathered pickup truck. Everything we smoke is done using traditional methods, utilizing an offset fire box for indirect heat and constant monitoring of temperatures at various points throughout the smoking chamber. True American barbecue is an art and always the result of time and experience. We use almost exclusively white oak for smoking, apart from the moments that benefit from tossing a bourbon barrel stave onto the fire. For mullet, as well as most seafood, I recommend a very mild wood. In addition to white oak, apple or pecan wood would also be appropriate.

The most important aspect of this recipe is "temperature." Creating and maintaining a consistent temperature of 225°F to 250°F is imperative. Given the application of the smoked fish and the recipe you intend to utilize it with, the fish could be cooked using an alternative method or temperature, assuming that the desired smoke flavor has been achieved. If the opportunity for a cold smoke (largely reliant on available equipment) exists, it would be ideal in many applications.

Our intention is to provide a resource for a fairly standard approach of brining the fish (which will season the fish, but also provide for a bit of insurance in a situation where the cooking temperature may be inconsistent) and the perspective of smoking in its basic form.

8 cups hot water

½ cup kosher salt

¼ cup granulated sugar

3 pounds fresh mullet fillets

Place the hot water in a large bowl. Add the salt and sugar, and whisk until completely dissolved. Allow to cool to room temperature. Place the mullet fillets in a shallow baking dish and pour the cooled brine over the top. Allow to sit for 1 hour, and remove the fillets from the brine onto a baking tray lined with paper towels.

To Smoke:

Place the mullet onto a small wire rack rubbed lightly with oil, and place into the smoker, ensuring the fish is located as far away from the heat source as possible. Smoke the mullet gently, at a consistent temperature of 225°F for 1¼ hours, or until the mullet has taken on a golden hue and the internal temperature of the fish is 185°F.

Note: Be sure to bring the temperature of the smoker up to cooking temperature (225°F) for a period of time prior to introducing the fish to ensure a consistent temperature environment.

RED ROCK CRAB BISQUE

SERVES 4-6

ALTERNATIVE FISH: BLUE CRAB, DUNGENESS CRAB, HIGH-QUALITY LUMP CRABMEAT

Every chef has an occurrence of an epic mistake, usually resulting in a large amount of waste. The effect of this "great loss" is internalized as a loss of time, effort, and energy, as well as respect from management and colleagues and always translates to a financial loss for the restaurant. In other words, the restaurant loses twice, both in the cost of the ingredients that were damaged and the cost associated with the loss of anticipated and potential sales.

My "great loss" was found during my formative years in the final moments of a two-day process meant to produce twenty gallons of lobster bisque while working at a historic restaurant in downtown Detroit. At the very last minute, just before finalizing the cooking process and eliminating the heat, I turned my back for a moment too long and the dairy scorched, immediately ruining the entire twenty gallons of terribly hard work.

If you're ever in the company of a chef, inquire as to their "great loss." If they don't respond immediately with a tale riddled with emotion and regret, they either haven't experienced it yet or they're lying.

For more information on red rock crab, see page 9.

Olive oil, as needed

5 pounds red rock crab shells

1 large onion, peeled and diced

2 medium-size carrots, peeled and diced

2 celery stalks, diced

2 tablespoons smoked paprika

1 teaspoon dried basil

1 teaspoon dried thyme

1 teaspoon dried oregano

1 teaspoon garlic powder

1 teaspoon kosher salt

¼ teaspoon cayenne pepper

16 ounces canned whole tomatoes in juice

8 cups Fumet (page 157)

4 cups heavy cream

3 sprigs fresh thyme

1 cup long grain rice

Sea salt, to taste

In a large stockpot, add enough olive oil to coat the bottom of the pot and place over medium-high heat. Add the rock crab shells and sauté until fragrant. Remove the shells from the oil and reserve for later. Add the onion, carrots, and celery, and sweat until softened, stirring occasionally, about 5 minutes. Reduce the heat to low, and add the smoked paprika, basil, thyme, oregano, garlic powder, salt, and cayenne pepper. Cook until fragrant, about 1 or 2 minutes. Add the tomatoes and cook until reduced by half. Add the Fumet, heavy cream, fresh thyme, and crab shells. Bring to a boil, and reduce to a simmer. Cook for 15 minutes and add the rice. Cook until the rice is tender. Remove the crab shells, purée well, and season with sea salt to taste.

Suggested Pairing

Marsanne/Roussanne Blend, Rhone, France

Marsanne and Roussanne are perfect blending companions. Where one lacks, the other has strength. Marsanne is full-bodied and earthy while roussanne is light and aromatic. Their complements combine to create wines that, with age, can be textured and nutty and, in their youth, austere and citrusy.

SPANISH FISHERMAN'S STEW

SERVES 4

ALTERNATIVE FISH: HALIBUT, HADDOCK, MAHI-MAHI, SEA BASS, SEA SCALLOPS

This recipe is generously provided by Rafel, the father-in-law of the incredibly talented food stylist, Emily, who spent her summer working with us in the kitchen as an intern. Emily went to Spain upon completion of her internship to travel, taste, and enjoy time spent with her partner's family, who resides there. When she returned from her adventures, she spoke of a beautifully humble stew prepared by Rafel, a fourth-generation fisherman from the village of Calafell. Rafel fishes every day, alone on his boat, without a crew. In the winter, he mends his fishing nets for the upcoming season, all of which he has made.

This recipe is created to make use of the monkfish, which once had no place in the market and was only brought home to feed the family of the fisherman who caught it.

For more information on monkfish, see page 6.

BROTH

½ pound monkfish (page 6), whole and gutted, cleaned

1 small onion, peeled and diced

2 stalks celery, diced

1 medium carrot, diced

6 cups water

GARLIC PURÉE

1 egg, room temperature

2 cloves garlic, peeled

½ cup oil

Sea salt, to taste

STEW

¼ cup olive oil

1 head garlic, peeled, divided

1 or 2 dry peppers, such as Piquillo

1 large slice of bread, cubed

½ cup white wine

2 pounds Yukon gold potatoes, small dice

2½ pounds monkfish fillet, cleaned and trimmed, large dice

1 cup short grain rice, such as Arborio

Sea salt, to taste

TO MAKE THE BROTH:

In a medium stockpot over high heat, add the monkfish, onion, celery, and carrot. Add enough water to cover by 1 inch. Bring to a boil, then reduce to a simmer, skimming any impurities that rise to the surface. Cook for 30 minutes, strain, and reserve.

TO MAKE THE GARLIC PURÉE:

Place the egg and garlic into a blender. Purée until smooth. Slowly add the oil, and season with salt to taste.

To make the Stew:

In a medium stockpot over medium heat, add the olive oil. Add half the garlic cloves and the pepper, and sauté until golden brown—do not burn the garlic! Remove the garlic and pepper and place into the bowl of a food processor or blender. Add the cubed bread to the oiled stockpot and sauté until golden. Place the bread into the blender with the garlic and pepper and add the wine. Purée until smooth, then transfer the mixture back into the stockpot. Whisk in the broth. Bring the mixture to a simmer and add the potatoes. Continue simmering until potatoes are tender, about 10 minutes. Strain the potatoes from the broth and set aside. Add the monkfish to the broth and simmer until cooked through. Strain the monkfish from the broth and reserve with the potatoes. Add the rice to the broth, and simmer until cooked through, about 15 to 20 minutes.

To Serve: Add the potatoes and fish back to the soup just before serving to heat through. Season with salt to taste, and garnish with the Garlic Purée.

SUGGESTED PAIRING

Cava, Catalynya, Spain

Spain's style of sparkling is made with the same techniques as the great Champagne region of France but with different grapes—a local blend of Macabeo, Parellada, and Xarel-lo grapes influenced heavily by the nearby Mediterranean. This wine is traditional at family celebrations of all types and served right alongside the regions' rich abundance of seafood.

ENTRÉES & SUPPER

Buttered Bread-Crusted Baked Amberjack 70

Citrus & Herb Infused
Salt-Baked Black Sea Bass 74

Pan-Seared Bluefish with Cellared Winter Vegetables &
Curried Butter Sauce 77

Citrus Honey Braised Cobia with Pumpkin and Fennel
Salad & Smoked Soy Cider Vinaigrette 82

Flounder à la Meuniere 86

Oven Roasted Grouper with Celery & Apple 90

Potato-crusted Haddock with Malt Vinegar Mayonnaise & Crisp
Pickled Salad ("Fish & Chips") 94

Pan-Seared Lingcod with Smoked Mussels, Roasted Fennel
Broth & Raw Fennel Salad 98

BUTTERED BREAD-CRUSTED
BAKED AMBERJACK

SERVES 4
ALTERNATIVE FISH: BLUEFISH, COD, MAHI-MAHI, SALMON, TUNA

This is an elegant opportunity to present a familiar combination of flavors and ingredients.
No one will have any idea their dinner plate contains a simple "tuna fish" sandwich. As for whether
to add mustard to this dish, the addition of mustard to tuna salad has appeared to be quite controversial
among my available resources. Therefore, we make the mustard flavors present and available to
those who subscribe to the mustard philosophy.

AMBERJACK

*The amberjack, which is a member of
the jack and pompano, is a popular
species inhabiting natural and man-
made reefs, rock outcrops, and wrecks
throughout Florida as well as the
Mediterranean, the Caribbean, South
America, and the Indo-Pacific.*

*Like many pelagic fish, the amberjack
is a voracious predator that forages
over reefs in small groups. Although
amberjack can grow quite large, it's
the smaller amberjacks, around fifteen
pounds or less, that make for the best
eating. Amberjack meat is white to
pale-pink, lean and mildly sweet,
with large flakes. It also has a firm
texture, which holds up well to various
cooking methods. When purchasing,
look for wild-caught amberjack as
opposed to the farmed variety. The
most sustainable amberjack are those
caught on hand lines or hook and line.*

*Although targeted by commercial
fishermen, the amberjack is
considered an incidental species when
hauled in on long-lines intended for
other more prized species such as
swordfish and tuna. They also make
up a percentage of bycatch
from gillnetters.*

4 (6-ounce) Amberjack fillet portions,
   skin removed

Kosher salt, as needed

Sugar, as needed

1½ cups Fresh Breadcrumbs (page 156)

⅛ teaspoon dill pollen

4 tablespoons butter, softened

6 tablespoons + ⅓ cup Garlic Shallot Mayonnaise
   (page 163), divided

Sea salt, as needed

2 heads butter Bibb lettuce

Linnea's Sweet Pickles (page 162), as needed

½ cup Sweet Pickled Pear Onions (page 173)

3 tablespoons Pickled Mustard Seeds (page 167) (optional)

At least 12 hours prior to cooking, marinate the fish using a dry brine of 50/50 (kosher salt/sugar) and allow to breathe in the refrigerator until ready to proceed. When seasoning the fish with the dry brine, don't be afraid to season liberally. Before cooking, dry the fish with paper towels to remove any excess moisture.

Preheat the oven to 400°F.

In a small bowl, combine the Fresh Breadcrumbs with the dill pollen. Add the butter into the mixture and combine until the butter is well incorporated and the breadcrumbs have a mealy texture.

Place the fish on a buttered baking dish, leaving room between the pieces to ensure even cooking. Spread 1½ tablespoons of Garlic Shallot Mayonnaise onto each piece of fish and top with the breadcrumb mixture, applying pressure downward to ensure the breadcrumb adheres to the top of the fish. Season lightly with sea salt and place into the oven.

Bake the fish for 16 to 18 minutes, or until the fish is firm and cooked to an internal temperature of 170°F and the breadcrumb mixture is golden brown. Remove from the oven and allow to cool.

TO SERVE: Place 1½ tablespoons of Garlic Shallot Mayonnaise at the front center of each plate and spread the mayonnaise across from front to back. Place a few torn leaves of butter Bibb lettuce off the center and place a piece of fish next to the lettuce. Garnish each plate with Linnea's Sweet Pickles (and some of the onions from the pickle jar) and Sweet Pickled Onions sliced in half.

SUGGESTED PAIRING

Helles Lager, Munich, Germany

Munich is the beer capital of the world. This lager-style beer is made with bottom-fermenting yeasts at colder temperatures with just a touch of hops, allowing for a fuller body and mild sweetness. Simple and understated, these styles of beer are crisp and refreshing.

CITRUS & HERB INFUSED SALT-BAKED BLACK SEA BASS

SERVES 2 OR 3

ALTERNATIVE FISH: ALASKAN BLACK COD/SABLEFISH, GROUPER, RED SNAPPER

Chef Gilles Renusson is responsible for inspiring and mentoring my early years through culinary school and my start in the industry. Always only a phone call away. Chef Gilles was available for the motivating words and perspective needed by a young cook making the many years of investment necessary to forge a future of leadership in the kitchen. One-hundred-hour work weeks were regularly met with the drive and encouragement from a whirlwind of French energy many miles away.

Upon the opening season of Salt of the Earth, Gilles dined with his wife while celebrating their wedding anniversary. I waited nervously in the kitchen while Gilles enjoyed his meal, dreading the response awaiting me from the service floor. It is assumed every chef will have a moment that will define his work and his craft, and an experience translated through the eyes of a mentor can serve as an ultimate perspective.

Once word came back from the floor, a slightly confused service member attempted to translate the words spoken through a thick French accent: "'A love affair' is what he keeps saying," mentioned the service member. Standing proud and tall, I made my way to Gilles's table, where he was beaming with energy. His smile spread from ear to ear. After a round of congratulations and a thorough endorsement, Gilles spoke of his comments that had made their way into the kitchen: "You, young man . . . have a love affair with salt . . ."

While Gilles's critique served as a reminder for the days ahead, we celebrate the following preparation in his honor.

BLACK SEA BASS

Black sea bass, which is actually a grouper, also goes by the name of rock bass, blackfish, or simply sea bass. These bottom dwellers, which prefer to congregate around rocks, man-made reefs, wrecks, piers, and jetties, can be found along the East Coast, such as off the coasts of North Carolina, Massachusetts, Florida, New Jersey, and Virginia. They are also abundant in the Gulf of Mexico. Black sea bass are highly sought after by recreational and commercial fishermen.

However, black sea bass accidentally caught in trawls and gill nets are considered a common bycatch species, while those landed by handline are deemed incidental catches when not being targeted specifically. For targeted black sea bass, new quotas are now in place to help limit overfishing. The mid-Atlantic shows good numbers of black sea bass, whereas the species is being overfished in the south Atlantic.

SIMPLE HERB PISTOU
2 cups flat-leaf parsley, minced

½ cup fresh chive, minced

3 garlic cloves, peeled and minced

1 medium shallot, peeled and minced

½ lemon, zested and juiced

¼ teaspoon red chili flakes

Extra-virgin olive oil, as needed

Fine sea salt, to taste

CUCUMBER SALAD
2 fresh cucumbers

6 ripe heirloom tomatoes (varied in size and color)

Olive oil, as needed

Smoked or coarse sea salt, as needed

BLACK SEA BASS
6 Caramelized Preserved Lemon slices (page 169)

3 fresh thyme sprigs

5 garlic cloves, smashed and peeled

4 pounds fine sea salt, divided

3 Meyer lemons, zested

4 tablespoons fresh thyme leaves

2 tablespoons black peppercorns, toasted and ground

4 farm-fresh egg whites

1 whole (2- or 3-pound) black sea bass, cleaned and scaled

Because of its small size, black sea bass is often prepared whole. The meat of the black sea bass is lean and firm, with small flakes and a mild, delicate flavor, making this fish easy to work with in the kitchen. Just be sure not to overcook this fish, which is easy to do because of its lean nature. As with all seafood, try and buy fresh rather than frozen whenever possible.

To make the Simple Herb Pistou:

In a small bowl, add the parsley, chive, garlic, shallot, lemon zest, and chili flakes. Mix well and add the olive oil to cover. Add the lemon juice when ready to serve. Season well with fine sea salt.

To make the Cucumber Salad:

Slice the cucumbers into ¼-inch slices and arrange on a platter. Slice, quarter, and halve the tomatoes depending on their size, achieving small to medium-size portions of varied shapes and sizes. Arrange the tomatoes with the cucumbers, and finish the platter with a drizzle of olive oil and sea salt prior to placing at the table.

To make the Black Sea Bass:

Preheat the oven to 450°F. Place the Caramelized Preserved Lemon slices, thyme sprigs, and garlic cloves into the cavity of the fish.

Place half the salt (2 pounds) into the bowl of a food processor and add the lemon zest, thyme leaves, and peppercorns. Pulse the salt mixture 5 or 6 times, or until the salt has broken down the aromatics. Remove the mixture from the processor and place in a medium-size mixing bowl. Add the remaining salt and

mix well to combine. Mix in the egg whites until thoroughly combined. The mixture should clump up if squeezed in your palm.

Grease a a high-sided baking sheet or baking dish large enough to hold the fish. Spread an even layer (½-inch) of salt onto the baking sheet, large enough to cover the profile of the fish. Mound the remaining salt over the fish and pack firmly, ensuring the salt fully encapsulates the fish. Place the probe end of an instant-read thermometer into the salt just under the back of the fish, below the fin (so you can register the temperature of the bottom fillet upon completion). Remove the thermometer, having used it simply to make a tiny opening.

Place the fish into the oven and roast for 20 to 22 minutes, or until the temperature of the fish reaches 175°F. Remove from the oven and allow the fish to rest for 10 to 15 minutes before presenting to the table. Garnish the platter with additional herbs and lemon slices.

Using the back of a wooden spoon, crack the crust and remove the salt chunk. Note: An additional plate or dish will be useful if doing this at the table. Also be mindful of the steam and heat escaping the cavity as you progress. Wipe the salt clean from the fish, and carefully peel back the skin of the fish. Discard the skin and flake portions of fish from the platter.

To Serve: Offer the fish "French style" to each guest, providing an ample amount of Simple Herb Pistou and a large platter of Cucumber Salad.

Suggested Pairing

Picpoul de Pinet, Languedoc, France

The oldest grape in the Languedoc has been thriving for centuries. This white wine provides soft and delicate textures, but is most well-known for its racy acidity (*piquepoul* translates as "lip-stinger"). This acid can neutralize strong salinity and provide a welcome pair to most crustaceans.

PAN SEARED BLUEFISH WITH CELLARED WINTER VEGETABLES & CURRIED BUTTER SAUCE

Serves 4-6
Alternative fish: Alaskan black cod/sablefish, amberjack, mackerel

Bluefish is a beautiful, hearty fish that allows for aggressive flavor pairings without losing its distinct characteristics. I love to prepare this moderately-flavored fish with curry spices, Vietnamese flavors, or fermented chilies. Bluefish also creates a perfect opportunity to provide a hearty offering while warming your guests, especially in the colder winter months. I recommend sourcing your root vegetables directly from the farmer and utilizing only the freshest toasted spices.

BLUEFISH

The bluefish is a popular gamefish, particularly on the east coast of the United States where they congregate off Florida in the winter and make their way north during the summer months in the waters off New York and Massachusetts. In the United States, most bluefish landed are by recreational fisheries. However, bluefish caught in gill nets, entangling nets, and bottom trawls by commercial fishermen are often considered bycatch when other pelagic species in the North Atlantic are being targeted. Bluefish are also caught and used for bait for larger sportfish like tuna, shark, and billfish.

The bluefish, with its broad, forked tail, steel-blue color, and razor-sharp teeth, is a ferocious predator that can grow upward of 30 pounds. It's also a one-of-a-kind fish, meaning they are the only living fish species of their family so nothing else in the ocean compares to it.

Bluefish do not live long; their average lifespan is around nine years. Nevertheless, they are very strong and aggressive during their short tenure in the ocean, attacking schools of squid, sardines, anchovies, and other smaller fish, including their own young, with quick bursts of speed known as the "bluefish blitz."

YOGURT MARINADE
2 cups plain yogurt

½ teaspoon ground cardamom

½ teaspoon garam masala

1 tablespoon freshly squeezed lemon juice

1 teaspoon Hungarian paprika

2 tablespoons tomato paste

2 teaspoons fresh minced garlic

1 tablespoon fresh grated ginger

WINTER VEGETABLES*
4 medium carrots, peeled or scrubbed

1 small pie pumpkin or squash

1 medium sweet potato, peeled

1 medium Yukon gold potato

1 large parsnip, peeled

Sea salt, as needed

BUTTER "CURRY" SAUCE
¼ cup extra-virgin olive oil

3 medium onions, medium dice (about 6 cups)

1 tablespoon kosher salt

5 tablespoons fresh grated ginger

15 garlic cloves, peeled and crushed

¾ teaspoon ground clove

1 tablespoon Hungarian paprika

2 teaspoons ground cardamom

¾ teaspoon cayenne pepper

¾ teaspoon ground cinnamon (Saigon)

2 tablespoons coriander seed, toasted

1 tablespoon granulated sugar

¾ cup lemon balm leaves

3¾ cups crushed tomatoes

3 cups water

¾ cup heavy cream

3 tablespoons unsalted butter

RAITA*
2 cups plain yogurt

2 green onions, sliced thinly

2 tablespoons fresh grated ginger

1 garlic clove, peeled and grated

1 cucumber, grated

1 lemon, juiced

1 teaspoon cumin seeds, toasted and ground

Sea salt, to taste

BLUEFISH
4–6 (6-ounce) bluefish fillets, cleaned and trimmed with skin on

Kosher salt, as needed

Granulated sugar, as needed

Cooking oil (e.g., vegetable, avocado, grapeseed), as needed

Fresh cilantro leaves, marinated onion, shaved cucumber curls, for garnish

Continued on page 79

To make the Yogurt Marinade:

In a medium-size mixing bowl, combine the yogurt, cardamom, garam masala, lemon juice, paprika, tomato paste, garlic, and ginger. Set aside.

To make the Winter Vegetables:

In a medium-size mixing bowl, add the vegetables and coat well in the Yogurt Marinade. Allow the vegetables to marinate for a minimum of 2 hours, but preferably overnight.

Preheat the oven to 400°F.

Remove the vegetables from the marinade and place into a colander to allow for the excess marinade to escape. Place the vegetables, spaced well, onto an oiled oven sheet and season well with sea salt. Roast the vegetables in the oven until lightly caramelized and tender, about 25 to 30 minutes. Remove from oven and set aside to cool.

To make the Butter "Curry" Sauce:

Place a 4-quart heavy-bottomed saucepot over medium-low heat for 1 or 2 minutes and add the olive oil. Add the onions and salt, and sweat until the onions are softened, about 4 to 5 minutes. Add the ginger and garlic, and sweat the garlic until softened, about 1 or 2 minutes, stirring often. Add the spices, sugar, and lemon balm, and continue to cook until fragrant, about 3 to 5 minutes. Add the tomatoes and water, then simmer until reduced by one-third. Remove from the mixture from the heat, and purée using an immersion blender or countertop blender. (Note: If using a countertop blender, allow for mixture to cool before blending, and do not overfill blender.) Return the puréed mixture to the saucepot over low-medium heat, and add the heavy cream and butter. Heat and stir the mixture until butter is melted and fully incorporated.

To make the Raita:

In a medium-size mixing bowl, combine the yogurt, green onion, ginger, garlic, cucumber, lemon juice, and cumin. Mix well and season to taste with the sea salt.

To make the Bluefish:

Pat the fish dry with a kitchen towel or paper towels. Season the fillets (thoroughly but not excessively) with a 50/50 mixture of the kosher salt and granulated sugar. Place the fillets into an appropriately sized dish and place in refrigerator for at least 2 hours.

Remove the fish from the refrigerator 30 minutes prior to cooking to allow the fish to come up in temperature. This will provide for even cooking of the fillet. Pat the fish dry using a kitchen towel or paper towel. Excess moisture on the fish will cause it to stick to the pan and may cause the fish to steam instead of sear.

Heat a large, heavy-bottomed sauté pan over medium heat until hot, about 3 to 4 minutes. Add enough cooking oil to just coat the bottom of the pan. Heat the oil for about 30 seconds before adding the fish. Place the fish skin-side down, laying the fish away from you and taking extreme care. Cook the fish until the bottom is golden brown and the fish releases easily from the pan, about 1 or 2 minutes. If fish seems to stick, it may need a short time longer. Carefully slide a fish spatula under the fish and flip to cook the remaining side. Remove from the heat when the color has turned throughout, and the flesh feels firm across the entire piece. Remove and sprinkle with sea salt after placing onto a paper towel–lined plate.

To Serve: In a medium-size bowl, spoon about ½ cup of the Butter "Curry" Sauce into the base of the bowl. Using a large slotted spoon, remove the roasted vegetables from the roasting tray, and place delicately over the sauce, arranging the vegetables by variety as you go. Place the bluefish over the vegetables, and dollop a heaping spoon of the Raita over the side or edge of the fish. Garnish with fresh cilantro leaves, marinated onion, or shaved cucumber curls.

SUGGESTED PAIRING

Riesling, Old Mission Peninsula, Michigan, USA

Nestled between the waters of Lake Michigan and Grand Traverse Bay, this region excels with grape varietals that enjoy a cooler climate. Winters can be harsh but the summer season can create Riesling of all types. The drier styles boast flavors of luscious tree fruits and tart apple.

CITRUS HONEY BRAISED COBIA WITH PUMPKIN AND FENNEL SALAD & SMOKED SOY CIDER VINAIGRETTE

SERVES 8-10
ALTERNATIVE FISH: SALMON, TUNA

The following dish is a fantastic opportunity to offer light and seasonally appropriate ingredients throughout the harvest season, which tends to be filled with heavy dishes and flavors. While presented here as a first course, the recipe can be thoughtfully prepared for a light lunch option.

For more information on cobia, see page 46.

CITRUS HONEY BRAISED COBIA

3 oranges, peeled and sliced

2 grapefruit, peeled and sliced

2 tablespoons Caramelized Preserved Lemon (page 130)

1 (2-inch) piece fresh ginger, peeled and sliced

1 stalk lemongrass, sliced

1 cup high-quality honey

1 cup neutral flavored oil (grapeseed is preferred)

1½ pounds cobia fillets

Smoked honey (optional)

Smoked sea salt

SMOKED SOY & CIDER VINAIGRETTE
Makes 1 cup

2 or 3 tablespoons barrel-aged smoked soy sauce

¼ cup apple cider

¼ cup high-quality honey

½ cup apple cider vinegar

PUMPKIN & FENNEL SALAD

1 small pie pumpkin, peeled, halved, and seeds scooped out

Extra-virgin olive oil, as needed

1 fennel bulb, stalks trimmed and fronds reserved

Continued on page 84

To make the Citrus Honey Braised Cobia:

In a blender or food processor, add the oranges, grapefruit, Caramelized Preserved Lemon, ginger, lemongrass, and honey, and blend until smooth. Slowly drizzle in the oil until completely incorporated.

Place the cobia fillets into a shallow baking dish. Pour the Citrus Honey marinade over the fillets, cover, and refrigerate overnight.

Remove the fish from the marinade, reserving the marinade.

Ensure the fish is very cold before proceeding. Remove any excess moisture from fish and oil lightly. Place oiled fish over intensely hot coals of a grill, or under a direct heat source such as a broiler (for tips on grilling, see page xxxi). Be mindful to char the exterior of the fish portions well, without causing an excess amount of cooking.

Place fillets and the marinade into a saucepot and place over medium heat. Once the marinade has come to a simmer, allow to cook for 8 to 10 minutes, or until the fillets are cooked through. Remove from heat, allow to cool in the liquid, and reserve in the refrigerator until well chilled.

To make the Smoked Soy & Cider Vinaigrette:

In a small bowl, add the soy sauce, apple cider, honey, and vinegar. Whisk well to combine and until honey is dissolved.

To make the Pumpkin & Fennel Salad:

Preheat oven to 375°F. Take one half of the pumpkin and dice into small cubes (about ½-inch, although consistency is more important than size). Toss in olive oil to coat, and spread in an even layer on a baking sheet. Roast in the oven until golden brown and cooked through, about 10 to 15 minutes, depending on the size of your cubes. Remove from the oven and reserve. Next, take the other half of the pumpkin, and with a vegetable peeler or mandolin, make paper-thin slices. Reserve. Cut the fennel bulb into quarters. Trim the root end and remove the core. Slice thinly on a mandolin or with a sharp knife. Toss the shaved pumpkin and shaved fennel gently in a small mixing bowl, dressing lightly with a touch of extra-virgin olive oil. Then season lightly with salt.

To Serve: Portion the chilled braised cobia into 1- or 2-bite portions, and place onto a serving platter. Assemble pieces of the roasted diced pumpkin around and over the cobia. Dress the fish and the platter lightly with the Smoked Soy & Cider Vinaigrette and top with small, pinched mounds of the Pumpkin & Fennel Salad. Finish with a drizzle of smoked honey and sprinkle of smoked sea salt.

Suggested Pairing

Unoaked Chardonnay, Santa Lucia Highlands, California, USA

Cold Pacific waters cast a fog bank that covers coastal California each summer season. The resulting "rain shadow" and highland vineyards help cool the normally hot days, and they help growing grapes achieve ideal ripeness. The unoaked versions of this varietal shine alongside citrus marinades and raw vegetables.

FLOUNDER À LA MEUNIERE

Every cook should have a full mastery of the foundational preparation *à la meuniere* (a French cooking term that literally means "miller's wife" and indicates flour is involved). The preparation is incredibly versatile and can have a quick application to just about any species of fish available. However you serve this flounder dish, focus on the cooking step of the fish and strive for perfection in its simplicity. I first encountered the à la meuniere approach at a historic classic French restaurant in Detroit, Michigan, using the flour and pan-sear method to cook Dover sole. The simplicity of the preparation allowed myself as a young chef to focus on the necessary nuances of heat and experience to result in a perfectly caramelized and perfectly cooked piece of fish. We continued the à la meuniere approach and concept to include another building block of French cuisine called *mirepoix*: the classic assembly of carrots, celery, and onion. Note that fish and Brown Butter (recipe below) pairs perfectly. Brown Butter, incidentally, is a magical preparation that baffles many new cooks in our kitchen. I often present them with the following challenge: "What is present in butter?" The answer is milk solids, butterfat, and water. Then: "What is present in cream?" The same response is intended. Cream has the same building blocks as the butter it creates, simply in a different form—a form perfect for creating this sauce. You'll be obsessed, we promise. This dish also pairs well with a fresh green salad that is simply dressed with fresh-squeezed lemon and olive oil.

FLOUNDER

There are many species of flounder that find their way to dinner tables across America, including Dover, English, starry and petrale. Soles, sanddabs, flukes, and plaice are also part of the flatfish family and may also be grouped into the "flounder" name.

Flounder, like all flatfish, are bottom-dwellers with wide, flat bodies and eyes on the top of the head, which enables them to see predators and prey while laying camouflaged on the muddy or sandy ocean floor. Because they feed on the bottom, flounders are very susceptible to bottom trawlers and bottom gill nets in which the flounder become bycatch when not being targeted specifically. When purchasing flounder, try to avoid those from the New England fishery or the US North and Mid-Atlantic. These areas have been overfished, while those flounders landed on the West Coast, particularly California and Alaska, are much more sustainable options.

FLOUNDER

1 large carrot, peeled and ends trimmed

4 (6-ounce) flounder fillets, cleaned and trimmed

2 cups all-purpose unbleached flour

4–6 ounces clarified butter or neutral-flavored oil (canola or grapeseed)

Kosher salt, as needed

Coarse flake or sea salt, as needed

Salt-Cured Celery (page 108)

Sweet Pickled Pear Onions (page 173)

To make the Flounder:

First, shave the carrot into long strips, using a French mandolin, Japanese mandolin, or simply a vegetable peeler. Place the carrot strips into a bath of ice water, and allow to chill for 10 to 15 minutes prior to serving. The carrot should curl into interesting shapes and curves. Dry well before plating.

Towel-dry the fish well prior to cooking. Place the flour in a large, shallow baking dish. Do not flour the fish until ready to cook.

BROWN BUTTER SAUCE
Makes ¾–1 cup

4 cups heavy cream

1 lemon, juiced

Fine sea salt, as needed

Continued on page 88

Place a large sauté pan over medium to medium-high heat. Allow the pan to heat for 1 or 2 minutes. Add the clarified butter or oil to the pan, and allow to heat for 30 to 60 seconds.

Season the fish well with the kosher salt, and dust immediately in the flour, being sure to remove any excess flour from the fish. Place the fish carefully into the hot pan. Once lightly golden brown, turn the fish using a fish spatula and finish cooking the other side. Remove the fish from the pan and sprinkle immediately with coarse flake salt.

To make the Brown Butter Sauce:

In a small, heavy-bottomed saucepot (3- or 4-quart), add the cream and bring to a boil. Note: the cream will easily "boil over" if not attended to, so stir the cream and reduce the temperature slightly to keep the cream from spilling over the sides of the pot. Continue to cook the cream at the highest manageable temperature, slowly reducing the moisture contained in the cream. As the cream thickens and reduces, decrease the heat to a simmer and continue to stir. The water content in the cream will continue to evaporate, and the remaining milk solids and butterfat will thicken further and then caramelize. Scrape the sides of the pot throughout, reintroducing the product to the cooking mass. Once the cream takes on a caramel tone, reduce the heat slightly and stir quite frequently. The thicker it becomes, the more likely the mixture will stick to the bottom of the pan and scorch or burn (ruining the preparation). Continue to cook the thickened mixture until deeply caramelized (dark-brown golden hue). Continue stirring frequently, removing any particles that have become stuck to the pan. Once the cream has thoroughly expelled its water content and is deeply caramelized, remove from the heat. Add the lemon juice while whisking aggressively to re-emulsify this mixture, and season with salt. Serve immediately. Note: Additional lemon juice is encouraged. Add more acid to achieve the balance of acidity and bite desired.

To Serve: Using a large spoon, place a few tablespoons of Brown Butter Sauce onto the center of a plate and push the spoon across the plate, front to back, drawing the sauce across as you go. Place a flounder fillet over the butter, just off center. Garnish the fish with the shaved carrot, Salt Cured Celery, and Sweet Pickled Onions.

SUGGESTED PAIRING

Pinot Grigio, Trentino, Alto Adige, Italy

Pinot Grigio is at home in the most northern grape-growing region in Italy. The grapes are grown on steep, often terraced, mountain vineyards and can provide lovely aromatic and crisp white wines with floral aromas that are a great match with delicate and flaky fish.

OVEN ROASTED GROUPER
WITH CELERY & APPLE

SERVES 8-10

ALTERNATIVE FISH: COD, HALIBUT, MONKFISH, SEA BASS, SNAPPER

I practice a philosophy in cooking intended to facilitate creativity and execution in organic experiences, building off foundational components and raw ingredients stocked in our larder, cellar, and pantry. As cooks and chefs, we attempt to find any opportunity to draw from our personal lives: the weather outside, the seasons surrounding us, as well as the ingredients that come through our back door. This drives our inspiration and allows for an emotional presence in our food. Purely magical moments are rarely the result of careful planning and organization.

I threw this dish together because of business partner Rob Nicol requesting "any kind of seafood." The result was a fresh fillet of grouper before being roasted next to the coals in a cast-iron skillet. Apples and celery felt appropriate with the delicate and subtle flavors of the grouper.
The Celeriac Purée is the perfect approach for many vegetables that may benefit from utilizing dairy as the cooking medium. The remaining flavorful cooking liquid can be used to adjust the consistency of the purée or reserved for a soup.

GROUPER

Grouper, with their compact body and large mouth used to swallow their prey whole, are a delicacy in many parts of the world, including the United States. These bottom dwellers can grow to considerable lengths and reach enormous weights, although the best eating groupers are of the smaller variety.

About 70 percent of the grouper harvested in US waters, particularly along the Florida coast and in the Gulf of Mexico, is the red grouper. Averaging 5 to 15 pounds in weight, it's the perfect size eating fish with white lean flesh and relatively few bones. The meat is often sold fresh and frozen as either whole fish, fillets, or steaks. The result after cooking is moist, firm meat with large flakes, similar to halibut. It also has a high oil content and its dense texture makes this fish very versatile in the kitchen. Many believe the red grouper is the best tasting among groupers. All groupers, incidentally, like species of tuna and swordfish, contain traces of mercury. Groupers can also carry Ciguatera, a foodborne illness caused by eating certain reef fish.

CELERIAC PURÉE

2 tablespoons salted butter

1 small to medium-sized onion, peeled and thinly sliced

Fine sea salt, as needed

2 pounds (2 or 3) medium-size celeriac, peeled and diced

Whole milk, as needed

3 or 4 tablespoons salted butter

GROUPER

2 (2-pound) grouper fillets, cleaned and trimmed

Olive oil, as needed

Smoked sea salt, as needed

½ stick butter

1 celery stalk

Roasted Apples (page 171)

Celery Vinaigrette (page 147)

TO MAKE THE CELERIAC PURÉE:

Heat a medium-size saucepot over medium heat. Add the 2 tablespoons of butter, allowing to melt slightly. Add the onion and a pinch of sea salt, and let sweat for 4 or 5 minutes or until softened and almost beginning to take on color. Add the celery root and cover with milk. Bring the pot to a boil and immediately reduce heat to a gentle simmer. Allow the celery root to cook until tender. Remove from heat, and strain off all cooking liquid, placing the remaining ingredients into the jar of a blender. Add additional butter; reserve the remaining for the Grouper. Purée until smooth and adjust seasoning with sea salt to taste.

TO MAKE THE GROUPER:

Preheat the oven to 450°F. Oil the grouper fillets well and place onto a baking sheet. Season well with the smoked sea salt and place into the oven. Roast the fish for 22 to 26 minutes, basting with the butter remaining from the Celeriac Purée during the final 4 minutes of cooking time. Meanwhile, prepare the celery garnish. Simply shave the celery stalk's entire length using a Japanese mandolin

Hawaiian, black, and gag groupers are several other best choices and the most sustainable when it comes to grouper consumption because, like red grouper, they're often hand-line caught. Because they may end up on hand-lines targeting other deep-sea fish, grouper can be classified as incidental catches. Groupers such as Warsaw, snowy, and yellowedge, on the other hand, are often considered bycatch, as they are typically landed by miles of long-lines set to catch other species.

Because mature grouper come together to spawn in large numbers, this makes them vulnerable to fishermen around the world. The exceptions are the red and black grouper from the US Gulf of Mexico, which are no longer overfished.

or vegetable peeler. Place the celery in ice water for a minimum of 10 minutes prior to serving. Press the fish's flesh to ensure it's cooked through, or insert a cooking thermometer to ensure an internal temperature of at least 165°F.

TO SERVE: Spoon the Celeriac Purée around the center of the plate in a circle, placing the grouper over the sauce. Arrange slices of Roasted Apples and garnish with the shaved celery. Finish with a drizzle of the Celery Vinaigrette. Note: You can also serve this dish with Sweet Pickled Apples (page 173).

SUGGESTED PAIRING

Chenin Blanc, Loire Valley, France

Chenin Blanc possesses a unique ability most white grapes do not: it can vary from dry to sweet, depending on region and winemakers' preferences. The Loire predominately produces dry Chenin Blanc that is crisp with fruit flavors of ripe apple, lemon peel, pear, and melon. This is a versatile pairing partner depending on the region, but look toward roasted fish and vegetables.

POTATO-CRUSTED HADDOCK WITH MALT VINEGAR MAYONNAISE & CRISP PICKLED SALAD ("FISH & CHIPS")

SERVES 6
ALTERNATIVE FISH: ALASKAN BLACK COD/SABLEFISH, AMBERJACK, MACKEREL

I couldn't bring myself to prepare the traditional representation of Fish & Chips. Instead, in representative style of our restaurant, I settled on a fun interpretation of the ingredients and components found in the traditional dish. As for the ramps, they are a wild spring onion and representative of one of our very first forgeable edibles in the spring. They are an absolute favorite of mine, and while only available for two to three weeks in the spring, we pickle and preserve as many bulbs as possible. Most seasons, we will process between 500 and 600 pounds of these incredibly flavorful wild-grown ramps for use throughout the remaining seasons. If not available, feel free to substitute with fresh pearl onions or the shaved white ends of a scallion.

For more information on haddock, see page 49.

HADDOCK

2 cups all-purpose flour

1 tablespoon Malt Vinegar Powder* (optional)

6 free-range or organic eggs

1½ cups Potato pearls or instant mashed potato flakes

½ cup potato flour (optional)

6–8 (4- to 6-ounce) cleaned, skinned, trimmed haddock fillets

Cooking oil (e.g., vegetable, avocado, grapeseed), as needed

Coarse sea salt, as needed

SALAD

8 baby dill pickles, quartered lengthwise

2 teaspoons capers (well rinsed)

4 medium/hard-boiled eggs, split and quartered

3 pinches of microgreens, or alternative small-leaf green such as watercress or arugula

8–12 pickled ramp bulbs

Extra-virgin olive oil, as needed

Coarse sea salt, as needed

SHAVED POTATO

¾ pound russet potato, peeled and held in water

Deep-fry oil, as needed

Fine sea salt, to taste

Malt Vinegar Mayonnaise (page 162)

*Note: Malt Vinegar Powder is available online or from most high-end spice purveyors. If not available, simply omit from the preparation.

TO MAKE THE HADDOCK:

Place the flour on a plate or shallow dish and distribute the malt vinegar powder throughout. Place the eggs into a similar container, ensuring the eggs have been thoroughly blended. In a third and similarly shallow container, place the potato flakes and mix well with the potato flour. Place each portion of haddock into the first container, coat thoroughly with flour, and shake off any excess before

Continued on page 96

moving the fish to the egg wash. Turn the fish through the egg, again ensuring a thorough coating before moving finally to the potato. Heap the potato flakes over and around the fish and pat lightly to ensure an even coating. Repeat with remaining portions.

Heat a large skillet over medium heat, and pour in enough oil to thoroughly cover the entire surface of the pan. Heat oil for 30 seconds, or until a tiny sprinkle of flour sizzles upon contact. Using extreme caution, lower each portion of fish into the pan, leaving space between the fish pieces. It is very important to not over-crowd the pan, as it may cause the fish to steam instead of panfrying. Be aware of the heat level, and moderate the burner to adjust the temperature as fish begins to cook. The crust will take on a crispy and golden exterior within 30 to 40 seconds of cooking. Turn the fish very carefully and continue the cooking process on all sides. Remove the fish from the pan, transfer to a wire rack or paper towel–lined dish, and sprinkle with coarse sea salt.

To make the Salad:

In a small mixing bowl, very gently combine the dill pickles, capers, hard-boiled eggs, microgreens, and pickled ramp bulbs. Drizzle with a small splash of olive oil and a tiny pinch of sea salt, if desired.

To make the Shaved Potato:

Shave the potato using a French or Japanese mandolin, with the blade set to facilitate a paper-thin slice of potato. As a general rule when using a mandolin, stop processing the ingredient at the point where your personal comfort level is affected by increased proximity with the blade. Alternatively, a vegetable peeler can be used to establish the shaved potato pieces needed.

Immediately transfer the potato shavings to clean water to prevent oxidization. Rinse and drain the collected potato shavings with multiple washes of water, until the drained water runs clear, having eliminated any excess starches that can contribute to a less than crispy result.

Using a stovetop deep-frying method of oil in an adequately sized pot and candy thermometer, or a dedicated deep-fryer, fry the shaved potato in batches at a temperature of 345°F. The lower frying temperature will allow for a gentle caramelization of the potatoes as they fry, as a higher temperature would cause the extremely thin potato slices to cook excessively quick.

Once the potatoes are well-fried and have taken on a thorough golden color, carefully transfer to a towel-lined dish and season well with fine sea salt.

TO SERVE: Place a heaping tablespoon of the Malt Vinegar Mayonnaise onto the plate and spread in a decorative fashion. Place a portion of the fish over the mayonnaise and top with the salad components. Garnish the plate with shaved potato.

SUGGESTED PAIRING

Sauvignon Blanc, Marlborough, New Zealand

New Zealand has only recently become an internationally recognized wine-producing region. Its success with the aromatic varietal Sauvignon Blanc pays tribute to its cool evenings and sun-laden days. Pacific winds howl through vineyards to keep the daytime heat at bay and keep the grapes on the vine, helping to raise sugar levels without sacrificing acidity. Look for notes of citrus and herbs to provide a great accompaniment to this seaside staple.

PAN-SEARED LINGCOD WITH SMOKED MUSSELS, ROASTED FENNEL BROTH & RAW FENNEL SALAD

SERVES 4-6
ALTERNATIVE FISH: BLACK COD, ROCKFISH

Before I moved to Fennville, Michigan, and opened Salt of the Earth, I was a part of the opening for Michael Symon's third restaurant, Roast. Located in Detroit's newly renovated Book Cadillac Hotel, a position at Roast was a personal achievement, as I had closely followed Michael's career from my early days in culinary school through the investment years that followed. I then ran the kitchen at Mabel's, Michael Symon's nationally acclaimed barbecue joint in Cleveland, Ohio, and met fellow kitchen colleague Bradley "Baller" Ball. We established a life long friendship that began with the smell of new stainless steel ovens getting their first round of natural gas and the polishing of freshly grouted quarry tile floors. Brad went on to operate the kitchen at Roast as executive chef and kept watch over the kitchen for all of us years after our exits. The following dish was one of Baller's first contributions to the menu at Roast. A terrifically simple winter dish, very much in spirit with some of the core lessons we all learned while working alongside Michael; strong, well-sourced ingredients presented simply.

LINGCOD

Lingcod is a commercially and recreationally important groundfish inhabiting the west coast of North America, with a strong abundance in Alaska. Because lingcod are overly aggressive predators that prey on virtually anything that swims, they grow fast and mature early, making them moderately resilient to fishing pressure. Although Alaska commercially targets lingcod using hook and line gear, many lingcod are accidentally caught by halibut and salmon fishermen, making the lingcod a common incidental and bycatch species. Nevertheless, the lingcod is considered a sustainable fishery, further proven by stable lingcod stocks.

Lingcod is available year-round, but the greatest appearance is in spring and summer. Lingcod is marketed as fresh or frozen, and consumers should know that lingcod meat often appears with a blue-green hue. Do not mistake this for spoiled fish. Unlike other white-meat fish, lingcod is unique in that its meat appears blue-green when raw but finishes white when cooked. It's also best to select smaller-size lingcod, as the giant (40 pounds and heavier) can be chewy and not as savory.

SMOKED MUSSELS
2 cups Fumet (page 157)

16–20 mussels (sustainably sourced and thoroughly cleaned)

ROASTED FENNEL BROTH
1 fennel bulb, split

Olive oil, as needed

Sea salt, as needed

½ pound mussel shells from Smoked Mussels, above

4 cloves garlic, smashed and peeled

1½ quarts Fumet (page 157), including the remaining steam broth from the mussels

1 pinch saffron threads

SHAVED FENNEL SALAD
½ bulb raw fennel, core removed

½ fresh lemon, zested and juiced

2 tablespoons finely minced flat-leaf parsley

1 tablespoon extra-virgin olive oil

LINGCOD
2 pounds lingcod fillet, trimmed and cleaned, skin on

Kosher salt, as needed

Granulated sugar, as needed

Cooking oil (canola or grapeseed), as needed

1½ sticks salted butter

Coarse flake salt, to season

The best and easiest ways to cook lingcod include baking, grilling, roasting, or searing.

To make the Smoked Mussels:

Heat the Fumet in a wide shallot pot until boiling. Add the mussels, cover with a lid, and allow the mussels to steam just until they open, about 2 or 3 minutes. Remove the mussels from the cooking liquid, discarding any mussels that did not open. Strain the liquid well and reserve along with the opened mussels.

Remove the mussels from their shells, and reserve the shells for the Roasted Fennel Broth. Smoke the mussels carefully and quickly, just briefly allowing them to garner some smoke flavor. For smoking specifics, see page xxxii.

To make the Roasted Fennel Broth:

Split the fennel bulb in half to reveal two broad halves. Oil the face of the fennel and char them thoroughly on an open grill or underneath the broiler (for tips on grilling, see page xxxi). The goal is a well-caramelized and roasted bulb on all faces. Remove from the heat source and allow to cool. Slice the bulb halves into long, thin strips and season with sea salt.

Next, heat a large cast iron pot or 6- to 8-quart pot over medium-high heat. Add 2 or 3 tablespoons of extra-virgin olive oil. Heat the oil for 30 seconds and add the charred fennel. Sauté for 1 minute. Add the mussel shells and roast them in the hot oil along with the fennel for another 1 or 2 minutes, or until well-toasted and caramelized. Add the garlic, followed by the Fumet and saffron threads. Let simmer slowly for 25 minutes. Remove from heat and strain well. Season with sea salt and reserve.

To make the Shaved Fennel Salad:

Shave the fennel into paper-thin pieces and place into a small mixing bowl. Add the lemon zest and juice, parsley, and olive oil, and toss well.

To make the Lingcod:

Pat the lingcod fillets dry with a kitchen towel or paper towels. Season well with a 50/50 mixture of kosher salt and granulated sugar. Place the lingcod into an appropriately sized dish and into the refrigerator (skin-side up) for two hours prior to cooking. Remove the lingcod from the refrigerator 30 minutes prior to cooking to allow the fish to come up in temperature. This will provide for even cooking of the fillet. Just prior to cooking, pat the lingcod dry using a kitchen towel or paper towel. Excess moisture on the fish will cause it to stick to the pan and may cause the fish to steam instead of sear.

Next, heat a large, heavy-bottomed sauté pan over medium heat until hot. Add enough cooking oil to just coat the bottom of the pan. Heat the oil for 15 to 30 seconds and add the lingcod fillets. Cook the fish until the bottom is golden brown and the fish releases easily from the pan. If fish seems to stick, it may need a short time longer. Carefully slide your fish spatula under the fish and flip to cook remaining side. Add the butter to the sauté pan and allow the butter to melt. As the fish cooks on the second side, using a large metal spoon, tilt the pan to allow for the butter to collect on one side. Spoon and baste the fish with the hot butter. Continue this basting throughout the remaining cooking time. Allow for caramelization of the fish and remove from the heat when the color has turned opaque throughout and the flesh feels firm across the entire piece. Remove and transfer to a paper towel–lined plate to rest. Season with coarse flake salt.

To Serve: Place one portion of the pan-seared lingcod (skin-side up) into the bottom of a shallow bowl. Carefully pour ½ to ¾ cup of the Roasted Fennel Broth around the fish. Place a few Smoked Mussels into the broth, and top with the Shaved Fennel Salad.

SUGGESTED PAIRING

Vermentino, Sardinia, Italy

Italy hosts a significant number of white wines of distinction. Vermentino,
home to the island of Sardinia, is one of the most well-travelled. Region
to region, it can garner different flavor and texture profiles, but the most
seafood-friendly styles are from Sardinia. Youthful with crisp, tart notes
followed by secondary characteristics of fresh herbs make these wines ideal
for broth-laden fish preparations.

FAMOUS PICKLE BRINED LIONFISH WITH CORNBREAD PURÉE & FRIED PICKLES

SERVES 2
ALTERNATIVE FISH: FLOUNDER, GROUPER, SNAPPER

The Gypsy Pig was an epic restaurant concept that served 250 folks per day at the peak of its operation. Located on the Christoffersen Family Farm in Fremont, Michigan, the eatery specialized in well-sourced farm-to-table fare. Orders were placed and received by bellying up to a 24-foot black walnut slab counter where crafted tales of the storied restaurant's past were relayed to hungry customers. The Gypsy Pig's logo was illuminated by night in lightbulb-lit letters and antique gooseneck fixtures to allow its patrons and guests to find it at any hour. The Gypsy Pig closed its doors on July 2, 2016, having served all guests in a 12-hour period, receiving not a single penny in exchange for its intensely thoughtful, handcrafted offerings. It should be noted that the restaurant was deemed one of the finest restaurants ever to open in West Michigan and regularly spoken of by the lifelong devotes of its existence.

For more information on lionfish, see page 52.

CORNBREAD PURÉE

1 cup cornbread, crumbled

¾ cup heavy cream

¼ cup buttermilk

½ tablespoon cream cheese

FRIED PICKLES

4 Dill Pickles (page 156)

¼ cup buttermilk

1 cup Country Dredge (page 153)

Deep-fry oil, as needed

Fine sea salt, to taste

PICKLE BRINED LIONFISH

1 quart water

3 tablespoons kosher salt

2 tablespoons sugar

½ tablespoon peppercorns, toasted

1 tablespoon coriander seed, toasted

¾ teaspoon red chili flakes

½ cup white distilled vinegar

8 garlic cloves, smashed and peeled

¼ teaspoon dill pollen

½ bunch fresh dill

¾ pound lionfish fillets, cleaned and portioned into 6-ounce pieces

TO MAKE THE CORNBREAD PURÉE:

To the bowl of a food processor, add the cornbread, heavy cream, buttermilk, and cream cheese. Purée on high for several minutes, until completely combined and thickened.

TO MAKE THE FRIED PICKLES:

Slice the pickles into ½-inch slices. Dip into the buttermilk, making sure to coat well. Remove each slice from buttermilk, and then place into the Country Dredge. Toss well to make sure all slices are evenly coated. Using a deep-fryer or large pot filled with oil over high heat, deep-fry the pickles for 45 to 55 seconds or until crispy and golden brown. Reserve on paper towels and sprinkle with fine sea salt.

To make the Pickle Brined Lionfish:

In a 4-quart saucepot, bring the water to a boil. Add the salt, sugar, peppercorns, coriander, chili flakes, vinegar, garlic, and dill pollen; whisk until the salt and sugar have completely dissolved. Remove the pot from the heat and allow to cool to room temperature. Add the fresh dill and pour over the lionfish fillets. Allow to sit for 1 hour, then remove lionfish from the brine. Grill the lionfish quickly over the intense heat of a natural hardwood lump charcoal grill (for tips on grilling, see page xxxi). Grill until fish is cooked through and reaches an internal temperature of 175°F.

To Serve: Place a large spoonful of Cornbread Purée in the center of each serving plate and top with a grilled lionfish portion. Place the Fried Pickles around the fish in a pleasant, random manner. It should be noted that pickled fish is best enjoyed in a quiet moment with someone you love, surrounded by hammocks strung from adjacent trees.

Suggested Pairing

Rioja Blanco, Rioja, Spain

Rioja is situated between the Atlantic and Mediterranean Oceans in Northern Spain. Its closeness to a high-elevation mountainous region helps isolate the area and provide a continental climate. Influenced by the French, traditional winemakers utilize new oak barrels to impart flavor and texture. Viura, Malvasía, and Garnacha blanca are the primary varietals used in blending and produce wines with ample texture and acidity with flavors of lemon curd, honey, and fresh herbs.

MACKEREL VERACRUZANA

Serves 4-6

Alternative fish: mullet, salmon, skipjack tuna

Thirty-some years ago, fellow restaurant owner Mark Schrock found himself on the shores of Veracruz, Mexico, with his wife, Martha, and then eight-year-old son, Jasen. A week-long residence on the Pacific coast followed, hammocks made up and occupied only feet from the rolling tide of the warm ocean water. In the coming days, and via the establishment of their "camp," a friendship was formed with fellow ocean hammock occupant Malachias, a local fisherman tasked with the duties of "scouting" for mackerel in a process of identifying the presence of schools of sardines, which would be followed by a run of mackerel and other predatory fish. On the third day of swapping stories hammock-side and sandy beach walks, Mark had the opportunity to launch the fisherman's heavy boats into the ocean once the telltale signs of a catch had presented themselves. Upon their return, Malachias shared a few mackerel with Mark to thank him for his help during the urgent boat launch. The departure from their beach camp led immediately to a feast facilitated by a backpacking stove, a few fresh ingredients from town, and a thorough cleaning and dressing of the mackerel, which was prepared using what was at hand: their motel room bathtub. Veracruz is a personal favorite with seafood. Quickly referenced from my early days in the kitchen with Mark, this fragrant and complex-flavored sauce is perfect in the summertime, served with fish hot off the grill—bathtub optional.

MACKEREL

In the southeastern United States, mackerel is often an incidental catch in both recreational and commercial fisheries. The two species most commonly caught in this region are king and Spanish mackerel. There is one population of Spanish mackerel, which is managed as two groups in the Gulf of Mexico and South Atlantic.

Spanish mackerel are coastal pelagic finfish. They prefer open water but are sometimes found over deep grass beds and reefs, as well as in shallow water estuaries. Spanish mackerel form large, fast-moving schools that migrate great distances along the shore. They feed on small fish, squid, and shrimp, often forcing schools of prey into crowded clumps and practically pushing the fish out of the water as they feed. Spanish mackerel grow to 37 inches and average 2 to 3 pounds. Fish older than five years are rare, though some females have been known to reach eleven years.

MACKEREL

6 whole mackerel, gutted and scaled

Olive oil (Spanish preferred), as needed

Sea salt, as needed

VERACRUZ SAUCE

Olive oil (Spanish preferred), as needed

2 medium-size sweet onions, small dice

Sea salt, as needed

1 small sweet pepper, cored, ribs and seeds removed, diced

1 fresh Fresno chili, ribs and seeds removed

6 garlic cloves, smashed and peeled

2 teaspoons whole coriander seed, toasted and coarsely ground

1 teaspoon red chili flakes (or de arbol chili)

5 medium/large fresh tomatoes or 2 (28-ounce) cans crushed tomatoes in juice

¾ cup green olives, roughly chopped

1 tablespoon fresh Mexican oregano (1 teaspoon dried Mexican oregano)

1 orange, zested and juiced (be sure to zest the orange before juicing)

1 tablespoon fresh cilantro, roughly chopped

TO MAKE THE MACKEREL:

Trim the fins and tail of the fish (they'll only burn when cooking) and coat well with olive oil. Season liberally with sea salt, and cook over the hot coals of a natural hardwood lump charcoal grill (for tips on grilling see page xxxi). Turn the fish gently halfway through once the skin of the fish is blistered and caramelized and the flesh is firm to the touch.

The slender, elongated body of the Spanish mackerel is silvery on the underside with a bluish or olive green back. Their distinguishing marks are the many small yellow and olive spots above and below the lateral line on both sides.

Spanish mackerel mature quickly and spawn prolifically, making them resilient to fishing pressure. However, juvenile Spanish mackerel are frequently caught as bycatch in the Gulf shrimp trawl fishery. Since a ban on gill nets in Florida state waters in 1995 was put in place, these fishermen have taken Spanish mackerel using hook-and-line gear, greatly reducing their catch. Because of these restrictions, Spanish mackerel are abundant in the Gulf of Mexico, and those from Florida should be requested.

Spanish mackerel are available fresh or frozen, whole, dressed, filleted, or as steaks. They are an excellent food fish—comparable to king mackerel, tuna, and mullet—with moderate texture and full flavor. Although suitable for frying, they are best broiled, baked, or smoked.

To Make the Veracruz Sauce:

In a large, enameled cast-iron pot set over medium heat, heat the olive oil. When hot, add the onions and season with sea salt (this encourages the onions' moisture to release quickly). Cook until the onions are softened and just about to take on color. Add the sweet pepper and Fresno chili. Add the garlic once the pepper is soft and slightly caramelized. Add the coriander and chili flakes, and cook briefly. Add the tomatoes, olives, oregano, and orange juice. Bring the mixture to a simmer, and cook for 18 to 20 minutes, or until 25 percent of the moisture has reduced. Note: This will be relative depending on fresh versus canned tomatoes. The adjustment in moisture necessary can be accomplished by using a bit of tomato juice, additional tomato (if early in the cooking process), or simply a bit of water. Season well with sea salt. Add the orange zest and cilantro juice before serving.

To Serve: Dress a large serving platter with a good amount of the Veracruz Sauce, and place the grilled mackerel on top. Dress the fish lightly with a bit of additional sauce, careful not to cover the fish, which would cause it to lose its perfectly crisp and blistered skin. Finish the platter with a few swipes of orange zest from a microplane and an extra drizzle of olive oil.

Suggested Pairing

Frappato, Sicily, Italy

Frappato is a grape growing in popularity with American palates. Native to the island, it is delicate and aromatic, but carries a fair amount of acid and tannin that allow it to be a wonderful food wine. Its aromatics are what makes it memorable, displaying scents of dried fruit and dried flowers. Light reds are a perfect match for rustic tomato- and pepper-based sauces.

PAN-SEARED MONKFISH WITH BEURRE BLANC, PICKLED POTATOES & SALT-CURED CELERY

SERVES 4-6

ALTERNATIVE FISH: GROUPER, HALIBUT, SEA BASS, SNAPPER

Upon a recent conversation with one of our guests at the restaurant who thoroughly enjoyed this dish, it was communicated to them that monkfish is sometimes referred to as "the poor man's lobster." The guest's response was perfect: "Well, for that price, I could have bought lobster." The butter sauce in this recipe gives this assertively textured fish a delicate and formal presence, perfect for a dinner party. I absolutely love to pair classic, time-honored preparations with monkfish. The fresh and crisp celery presents a perfect contrast to the fat in the butter, the acid in the sauce, and the saltiness of the capers, anchovies, and cured celery.

For more information on monkfish, see page 6.

SALT-CURED CELERY
4 celery stalks, trimmed

Olive oil, as needed

Kosher salt or fine sea salt, as needed

FRESH-SHAVED CELERY
2 celery stalks, trimmed and leaves removed

PICKLED POTATOES
6–8 medium Yukon gold potatoes

Water, to cover

½ cup distilled white wine vinegar

½ cup apple cider vinegar

½ cup granulated sugar

CAPER ANCHOVY SAUCE
¼ cup capers, rinsed well to remove excess salt

4 salt-packed or olive oil–marinated anchovies

½ tablespoon fresh shallot, peeled

¼ tablespoon fresh garlic, peeled

1 tablespoon fresh minced flat-leaf parsley

Zest of ½ lemon

¼ teaspoon red chili flakes

Fine sea salt, to taste

Extra-virgin olive oil, as needed

¼ lemon, juiced

MONKFISH
4–6 (6–8 ounces each) monkfish fillets, cleaned and trimmed

Kosher salt, as needed

Granulated sugar, as needed

2–4 tablespoons cooking oil (e.g., vegetable, avocado, grapeseed)

1½ sticks salted butter

Sea salt, to taste

BEURRE BLANC SAUCE*
3 sticks cold salted butter, diced into chunks

1 tablespoon minced shallots

¼ cup dry white wine

¼ cup white wine vinegar

1 tablespoon fresh-squeezed lemon juice

Fine sea salt, to taste

*This classic white butter sauce requires a bit of focused whisking as well as a strong intuition of heat levels while constructing. Make it once and you'll have a difficult time pairing seafood with any other sauce. It's quite addictive.

Continued on page 110

TO MAKE THE SALT-CURED CELERY:

Cut the celery on a long bias to achieve a piece that is 1½ inches in length, and ¼-inch thin. Add the celery pieces to a small mixing bowl, and coat well with olive oil. Season liberally with salt. Place in a vacuum seal bag, and seal using a vacuum sealer (or simply add to a ziptop bag, removing all the air out of the bag). Allow to sit for minimum of 1 hour, ideally overnight.

TO MAKE THE FRESH-SHAVED CELERY:

Using a vegetable peeler, draw across each celery stalk to achieve long ribbons of celery. Place the shaved celery pieces into a small container and cover fully with cold water. Place into refrigerator until ready to use.

TO MAKE THE PICKLED POTATOES:

Slice the potatoes into coins, about ¼-inch thick. Place the potatoes into a small saucepot, and cover with water, just to submerge. Bring up to a simmer, cover, and cook for 15 minutes. Add the vinegars and sugar, and continue to cook the potatoes until tender, about another 10 to 15 minutes.

TO MAKE THE CAPER ANCHOVY SAUCE:

Using a food processor or simply a chef's knife and a cutting board, mince the capers extremely fine along with the anchovies, and place into a small mixing bowl. Mince the shallot and garlic and add to the bowl, along with the parsley, lemon zest, and red chili flakes. Season well with the sea salt, and mix the ingredients well until combined. Add the olive oil just to cover the ingredients and mix well. When ready to serve, add the lemon juice.

TO MAKE THE MONKFISH:

Pat the fish dry with a kitchen towel or paper towels. Season the fillets (thoroughly but not excessively) with a 50/50 mixture of the kosher salt and granulated sugar. Place the fillets into an appropriately sized dish and place in refrigerator for at least 2 hours.

Remove the fish from the refrigerator 30 minutes prior to cooking to allow the fish to come up in temperature. This will provide for even cooking of the fillet. Pat the fish dry again using a kitchen towel or paper towel. Excess moisture on the fish will cause it to stick to the pan and may cause the fish to steam instead of sear. Heat a large, heavy-bottomed sauté pan over medium heat until hot, about 3 to 4 minutes. Add enough cooking oil to just coat the bottom of the pan. Heat the oil for about 30 seconds before adding the fish. Place the fillets in the pan, laying the fish away from you and taking extreme care. Cook the fish until the bottom is golden brown and the fish releases easily from the pan, about 1 or 2 minutes. If fish seems to stick, it may need a short time longer. Carefully slide a fish spatula under the fish and flip to cook the remaining side. Remove from the heat when the color has turned throughout, and the flesh feels firm across the entire piece. Next, add the butter and let melt. As the fish cooks on the second

It is imperative that you use an appropriately large sauté pan when searing fish at high heat or cooking fish in batches. You must provide an adequate amount of space between the individual pieces to ensure a consistent temperature of the pan, as each addition of fish will in effect cool the pan and drop the temperature of the sauté pan as it responds to the cold temperature of the fish. Overcrowding the pan will cause the temperature to drop excessively and result in the fish sticking and subsequently steaming instead of searing.

side, using a large metal spoon, tilt the pan to allow for the butter to collect on one side, collect the butter with the spoon, and baste the fish with the hot butter. Continue this basting throughout the remaining cooking time. Remove the fish and sprinkle with some sea salt after placing onto a paper towel–lined plate.

To make the Beurre Blanc Sauce:

Place a heavy-bottomed 2-quart saucepot over medium heat and add 1 or 2 small, diced pieces of butter into the pan. Allow the butter to melt. Once it begins to bubble slightly, add the shallots. Stir the shallots and cook quickly until translucent, but do not allow the shallots or the butter to develop any color. Add the dry white wine and the white wine vinegar to the shallots, and allow to reduce until the liquid has reduced and is almost fully evaporated. Reduce the heat to very low, and move the saucepot off the burner until only a small portion of the pot is over the burner. Add a few more small pieces of the diced butter into the pot and, using a small whisk, move the butter throughout the mixture to emulsify it as it melts. Once the initial butter has melted, add a very small amount of additional butter and continue the process. Run the finished sauce through a small, fine strainer, if desired. Finish the sauce with the fresh lemon juice, and season well with the fine sea salt. Serve immediately.

To Serve: In a bowl or shallow-rimmed plate, spoon 3 or 4 tablespoons of the Beurre Blanc into the center of the dish. Place a small pile of the warm Pickled Potatoes on one half of the dish. Place 4 or 5 pieces of the Salt-Cured Celery over and around the potatoes. Spoon small piles of the Caper Anchovy Sauce around and over the potatoes. Place the monkfish onto the potatoes and garnish with the Fresh-Shaved Celery, removing all excess moisture from the celery prior to plating.

Suggested Pairing

Chardonnay, Burgundy, France

The Côte de Beaune region of Burgundy is the ancestral home to the Chardonnay grape and provides the world with unparalleled examples of the variety. New oak usage can push prices but also create wines that integrate weight and flavor. Look for notes of warm spice, toasted bread, and golden apple. Perfect with meaty fish and rich, cream-based sauces.

WHOLE ROASTED PORGY WITH SWEET CORN, MARINATED POLE BEANS & WINTER SQUASH

SERVES 4

ALTERNATIVE FISH: OCEAN PERCH, RED SNAPPER, ROCKFISH

West Michigan Native Americans would fertilize the soil for the spring season by burying whole porgies in mounds of dirt, upon which they would revisit in the spring and plant corn seed, progressing to pole beans, and finally to winter squash. They grew these crops together and established the method of "companion planting": varieties of vegetables that benefit from the growth of others. In this case, the corn serves as a natural support system for the pole bean to climb, the beans provide nitrogen for the soil (which has been depleted by the corn), and the squash provides ground cover for the first two, eliminating the opportunity for weeds to flourish and draw nutrients away from the surrounding crops.

We celebrate the fall tradition of "planting" fish to enrich the soil for the upcoming growing season in our own garden, and in doing so, give back what we took during harvest. We also take the opportunity to roast the porgies whole next to the wood fire, serving them with their "Three Sisters," preserving the corn so that it may be available to enjoy alongside the relative components.

PORGY

Native to the Atlantic Ocean, porgy, considered the "red snapper of the Northeast" by local fishermen, is a general term for several species belonging to the Sparidae family. Sea bream, sheepshead (not to be confused with the California sheepshead), and scup are three Sparidae species commonly referred to as porgy. Otter Trawlers, targeting more commercially viable species, often catch their fair share of porgy as bycatch. Fortunately, fishing practices have improved and porgy populations are better than they used to be.

Because Porgy are relatively slow swimmers, small, and easy to catch, they also often end up as incidental catches—and then used as bait— especially among recreational fishermen in shallow water. Anglers on the East Coast, for example, often land porgy when trying to target fluke or striped bass.

Similar to red snapper in texture and taste, porgy, which is often sold whole due to their small size, is a white-fleshed, medium-fatty, not too lean or oily fish with a sweet, delicate flavor.

MARINATED POLE BEANS
½ pound dried black turtle beans (or similar black bean)

1 cup red wine vinegar

2 tablespoons sugar

2 tablespoons kosher salt

Juice of 1 lime

1 tablespoon dark chili powder

1 teaspoon New Mexico powder (or similar ground chili powder)

1 teaspoon Guajillo chile powder (or similar ground chili powder)

1 teaspoon smoked Serrano powder (or similar ground chili powder)

PRESERVED SWEET CORN
Kernels of 8 ears of corn

1 cup white wine vinegar

1 cup water

2 tablespoons sugar

1 tablespoon kosher salt

1 teaspoon mustard seeds

1 teaspoon toasted black peppercorns

1 teaspoon toasted coriander seed

CORN CAKES
2 farm fresh eggs, separated

1 cup corn kernels

¼ cup green onion, thinly sliced

2 tablespoons vegetable oil

¼ cup all-purpose flour

¼ cup cornmeal

¼ cup butter, for cooking

Kosher salt, as needed

SHAVED SQUASH SALAD
1 winter squash (1 or 2 pounds), such as hubbard, kabocha, or acorn

1 ounce white wine vinegar

1 teaspoon freshly ground black pepper

2 teaspoons honey

⅛ teaspoon smoked Spanish paprika

2 ounces olive oil

1 tablespoon toasted pumpkin seed oil

Continued on page 114

Despite their name, which was American Indian for "fertilizer," many consumers enjoy their flavor and panfish size, which makes them suitable for easy frying, broiling, and baking.

PUMPKIN PURÉE

1 pie pumpkin (2 or 3 pounds)

Olive oil, as needed

Sea salt, as needed

1 cup apple cider

1 cup water

2 sprigs fresh thyme

1 tablespoon honey

1 tablespoon white vinegar

PORGIES

4 whole dressed porgies, scaled and trimmed

Olive oil, as needed

Sea salt, as needed

TO MAKE THE MARINATED POLE BEANS:

Soak the beans overnight in enough cold water to cover by 3 inches. When beans are fully hydrated, drain and place in a large pot. Add enough water to cover by 2 inches. Place the pot over medium-high heat, bring to a boil, and reduce heat to a simmer, cooking the beans until tender. Allow the beans to cool in the cooking liquid. Once beans are cool, strain the cooking liquid off and discard. Place the beans into an appropriately sized container. In a smaller saucepot, add the vinegar, sugar, salt, lime juice, and chili powders. Bring to a boil, stirring to dissolve all the ingredients. Pour the hot liquid over the beans, cool, and reserve.

TO MAKE THE PRESERVED SWEET CORN:

Place the corn kernels in a large bowl and set aside. In a small saucepot, add the vinegar, water, sugar, salt, mustard seeds, pepper, and coriander seed. Bring to a boil over high heat, stirring to dissolve all the ingredients. Pour the hot brine over the corn kernels, then allow to cool and reserve. Note: Be sure to save your corn cobs for use in a quick and versatile Sweet Corn Stock (page 172).

TO MAKE THE CORN CAKES:

Place the egg whites in a 2-quart bowl, and allow to warm to room temperature. Whip the egg whites to soft peaks, taking care not to overwhip. Next, place the corn into the bowl of a food processor. Pulse gently until corn is lightly puréed. Add the egg yolks, green onion, and oil, and mix until smooth. Place the corn mixture into a large mixing bowl, and add the flour and cornmeal in multiple additions, incorporating well. Mix until smooth. Very gently fold in the egg whites, turning the corn mixture over to incorporate the egg whites. Be patient and resist the urge to overmix.

Heat a sauté pan over medium heat. Add 1 tablespoon butter and allow to melt. Using 2 large tablespoons, drop a heaping tablespoon of batter into the pan, and repeat until the pan is full, leaving 1 inch of space between each cake. Cook until golden brown and flip with a spatula, cooking on the opposite side until golden.

Continued on page 116

When cakes are cooked, remove to a baking tray lined with paper towels. Season with sea salt, if desired. Repeat this process until all the batter is used. Once the corn cakes have adequately drained, remove the paper towels to ready the pan for reheating.

Note: Feel free to make the corn cake as large as desired by altering the amount of batter placed into the pan at a time, simply ensuring that you spread the increased volume of batter across the cooking surface to a thickness of ½ inch.

To make the Shaved Squash Salad:

Carefully cut the top and bottom of the squash. Peel the rind with a vegetable peeler and discard. Halve the squash and scoop out the seeds, reserving for later. Scrape the squash clean of stringy pulp. Cut each half into quarters. With a vegetable peeler (or mandolin), shave the squash into long, thin strips. Rinse the shaved squash well by placing in a container and covering with cold water. Drain and repeat process 3 or 4 times. Place into a medium-size mixing bowl.

In a separate small mixing bowl, add the vinegar, pepper, honey, paprika, and olive oil, and whisk well to combine. Pour the vinaigrette over the squash and toss well to coat completely. Allow to marinate for at least 30 minutes. Finish with the toasted pumpkin seed oil prior to serving.

To make the Pumpkin Purée:

Preheat the oven to 375°F. Carefully cut the pumpkin in half. Scoop out the seeds and pulp, and discard. Rub one half of the pumpkin with olive oil and season well with sea salt. Place onto a baking tray and roast in the oven until tender. Remove from the oven, allow to cool, scoop out the flesh, and reserve.

Next, peel the remaining pumpkin half, and dice into 1-inch pieces. Heat a large pot or Dutch oven over medium-low heat. Add 2 tablespoons olive oil and the pumpkin. Cook the pumpkin until slightly softened, and add the apple cider and water. Bring to a simmer, add the thyme sprigs and roasted pumpkin, and cook until diced pumpkin is tender, about 30 minutes. Remove the thyme. Allow the pumpkin to cool slightly, and place in a blender, taking care to only fill the blender halfway. Blend until smooth, place in a mixing bowl, and repeat with remaining pumpkin mixture. Whisk the batches together in the mixing bowl to combine, and add the honey and vinegar. Mix well and season to taste with sea salt.

To make the Porgies:

Preheat the oven to 500°F. If necessary, trim all the fins and tail from the fish, if desired (they will simply burn during the cooking process). Cut 3 to 5 slits onto both sides of the fish, not penetrating too deeply with your knife (a very sharp knife is necessary here). The goal is to simply score the skin. Dress the fish well with olive oil, and season well with salt, distributing thoroughly into the slits and skin of the fish. Place on a baking sheet, and roast the fish for 18 to 22 minutes, checking every 3 minutes once 12 minutes have elapsed. Once fully cooked, the flesh of the fish should be firm and bright white. Remove from the oven and allow to cool. Note: If the fish is fully cooked, but lacking in char and blister, place under the broiler very briefly after the fish has cooled to enhance visual serving appearance.

To Serve: Place a large spoonful of the Pumpkin Purée just off center on a serving platter. Place the Corn Cakes at the center of the plate, and place the Porgies beside the cakes, opposite of the Purée. Top the underside of the fish with a pile of the Shaved Squash Salad. Place several spoonfuls of the Marinated Pole Beans around the plate. Drizzle the dish with a bit of toasted pumpkin seed oil to finish.

Suggested Pairing

Pinot Noir, Central Otago, New Zealand

New Zealand is hands down one of the most beautiful, unique, and varied wine regions in the world. Central Otago sits more inland than any other wine-producing region, boasting a continental climate that allows the fickle Pinot Noir grape to excel. Delicate but lush fruit joined with a fine tannin structure make this wine a suitable pairing partner for seafood with savory applications.

COUNTRY-FRIED REDFISH WITH MUSTARD PICKLED POTATO SALAD & HERBED BUTTERMILK VINAIGRETTE

SERVES 4
ALTERNATIVE FISH: BLACK SEA BASS, GROUPER, HADDOCK, MONKFISH

Nothing delivers the flavors and memories of a hot summer day better than a Southern country fish fry, particularly fresh redfish, along with homemade potato salad and a bright and acidic buttermilk vinaigrette loaded with a garden full of herbs.

REDFISH

Redfish, not to be confused with certain species of rockfish, are also known as red drum or channel bass, and are a respected inshore game fish found in the Atlantic Ocean and in the Gulf of Mexico, as well as in bays and estuaries in many southern states, such as Louisiana and Texas. They are a schooling species and a strong fighter when hooked. Despite not being targeted by commercial fishermen, redfish, which are often considered an incidental catch when not being fished for sport, are appearing more and more on restaurant menus across the country because of their excellent flavor.

Today, redfish are also being farmed in ponds across the United States. Although the farmed variety is a better alternative when it comes to seafood sustainability, there's something to be said for plucking a young redfish from the wild. The mild, sweet flavor and moist white meat seems to be far superior, especially from those smaller redfish less than 10 or 15 pounds, as the meat of larger "bull" redfish can be coarse, stringy, and unpalatable. Both the redfish and its cousin, the black drum, have similar flavors, with the redfish having a finer texture and more tender, flaky flesh.

Because redfish may contain parasites, it's recommended that the fish always be cooked through and not served raw for sashimi or ceviche.

MUSTARD PICKLED POTATOES
2 pounds fingerling or other small potatoes

1½ teaspoons dry mustard powder

1½ tablespoons Dijon mustard

1½ teaspoons turmeric

2½ cups water

1¼ cups white distilled vinegar

¾ cup granulated sugar

1½ tablespoons kosher salt

PICKLED POTATO SALAD
Mustard Pickled Potatoes

Celery Verde (page 147), as needed

1 large bunch watercress, or alternative spicy hearty green, picked through and thick stems removed

Buttermilk Vinaigrette (page 143)

REDFISH
Country Dredge, as needed (page 153)

4 farm-fresh pastured eggs, blended

1 tablespoon hot sauce (Frank's Red Hot)

4 (6-ounce) redfish fillets, cleaned and trimmed

1½ cups lard (or substitute with frying oil)

Coarse sea salt or flake salt, as needed

TO MAKE THE MUSTARD PICKLED POTATOES:

Add the potatoes to a medium stockpot. Pour enough water to cover the potatoes by 1 inch. Place the pot over medium-high heat and bring to a boil. Lower heat to a simmer, and cook until the potatoes are tender. Strain, then allow to cool.

In a medium saucepot over high heat, add the dry mustard, Dijon, turmeric, water, vinegar, sugar, and salt. Whisk to combine. Bring to a boil, ensuring all the ingredients are dissolved. Remove from heat. Transfer the cooled potatoes to a container with at least 2 inches of clearance. Pour the hot brine over the potatoes, and allow to marinate in refrigerator for a minimum of 2 hours.

Continued on page 120

TO MAKE THE PICKLED POTATO SALAD:

In a medium bowl, toss the chilled Mustard Pickled Potatoes with some Celery Verde and watercress.

TO MAKE THE REDFISH:

Place the Country Dredge into a medium-size shallow container. Do the same with the egg mixture, seasoned with the hot sauce. Thoroughly dry the fish fillets, and place into the Country Dredge, ensuring an even and thorough coating of the mixture. Place each dredged fillet into the seasoned egg mixture, again ensuring an even coating before transferring back to the Country Dredge one final time. Keep the fillets in the Country Dredge until ready to fry.

To panfry: Melt the lard or heat the oil in a large sauté pan or cast iron skillet over high heat. Once the fat has reached a temperature of 375°F, gently and carefully place the fish into the hot fat. Fry the fish for 2 or 3 minutes or until golden brown and crispy. Turn the fish over to finish cooking. Cook for an additional 2 minutes and remove from the lard and place on a plate lined with paper towels. Sprinkle with coarse sea salt or flake salt.

TO SERVE: Paint the plate with some Buttermilk Vinaigrette. Place a piece of the fried redfish off center on the dressing, and garnish with a heaping scoop of the Pickled Potato Salad.

SUGGESTED PAIRING

Pinot Blanc, Alsace, France

Alsace is a picturesque wine region on the eastern boarder of France. It is blessed with great soil, wonderful climate, and noble grape varieties. Pinot Blanc presents a vivid nose of apple and pear with a medium body and light acidity. A great accompaniment to any light seafood preparation.

FRIED REDFISH WITH SWEET CORN & CRAB SAUCE

SERVES 6-8

ALTERNATIVE FISH: BLACK SEA BASS, GROUPER, HADDOCK, MONKFISH

Salt of the Earth cofounder Steve Darpel spent many of his adolescent years mopping floors, washing dishes, and later tending bar at his family's corner bar Darpel's Cafe in Covington, Kentucky. Upon presenting the first draft of our opening menu for Salt of the Earth in 2009, Steve mentioned his desire for a dish that would represent one of the most celebrated offerings of Darpel's Café, which stood the test of time throughout every resulting passage of the neighborhood corner bar to the next generation—The Friday Night Fish Fry. This sweet corn and crab "salad" is the perfect accompaniment for summertime fried fish. Incredibly simple and insanely delicious, we celebrate the opportunity to relish in the season with friends and family all while thoroughly endorsing our chanting of "TGIF!"

For more information on redfish, see page 118.

For more information on red rock crab, see page 9.

REDFISH

2 pounds redfish fillets, cleaned and trimmed

Kosher salt, as needed

Granulated sugar, as needed

2 cups Country Dredge (page 153), or seasoned all-purpose flour

High-heat oil (canola or peanut) or vegetable shortening

Sea salt, as needed

SWEET CORN & CRAB SAUCE

1½ tablespoons olive oil

1 cup salted butter, diced, divided

1 medium-size shallot, peeled and finely minced

½ red Fresno chili, seeds and ribs removed, finely minced

½ jalapeño pepper, seeds and ribs removed

3 gloves garlic, peeled and finely minced

Kosher salt, as needed

4 ears organic sweet corn, kernels removed (reserve the cobs to make the Sweet Corn Stock)

2 cups Chicken Stock (page 149)

6 fresh lemons, zested and juiced (about 10 ounces juice)

1 cup Sweet Corn Stock (page 172)

½ pound red rock crabmeat

⅓ cup minced chives

TO MAKE THE REDFISH:

Two hours prior to cooking the fish, pat the fish dry with a kitchen towel or paper towels. Season thoroughly with a 50/50 mixture of the salt and sugar. Transfer the fish to an appropriately sized dish and place in refrigerator until ready to proceed.

Remove the redfish from the refrigerator 30 minutes prior to cooking to allow the fish to come up in temperature. This will provide for even cooking of the fillets. Pat the fish dry using a kitchen towel or paper towel. Excess moisture on the fish will cause it to stick to the pan and may cause the fish to steam instead of sear.

Place the Country Dredge into a shallow container, and place the fish fillets into the mixture, one by one, ensuring a thorough coating of the Dredge to every surface of the fillets. Allow the fish to remain in the mixture long enough to absorb an appropriate amount of the dry mixture. Shake off any excess.

Next, heat a large, high-sided pan with ½ inch of the oil over medium-high heat. Heat the oil to a consistent temperature of 375°F (check with an instant-read thermometer) and carefully place a moderate amount of fish into the oil at a time (this is dependent on how large your cooking pan is). Note: Do not place too much fish into the oil at once, as the temperature will drop significantly, eliminating your ability to appropriately perform the frying function. Cook the fish for 1 to 1½ minutes on each side or until golden brown and crispy. Carefully remove the fried fish from the hot oil and transfer onto a paper towel–lined dish or wire rack. Season with sea salt.

To make the Sweet Corn & Crab Sauce:

Heat a large, heavy-bottomed stainless steel sauté pan over medium heat. Allow the pan to heat for 1 or 2 minutes, and add the olive oil and 2 tablespoons of the butter. Once the butter has melted, add the shallot and cook briefly while stirring constantly. Add the minced chilies and garlic and cook for an additional 30 seconds. Season well with kosher salt. Add the corn to the hot pan and sauté for 1 minute to allow the corn to caramelize slightly. Add the Chicken Stock, lemon zest and juice, and Sweet Corn Stock, and bring to a boil. Allow the mixture to reduce heavily, until 90 percent of the moisture has been evaporated. Add the crabmeat and mix gently to incorporate. Once the crab has been moderately heated, remove the pan from the heat and incorporate the remaining butter little by little. Season again with salt. The resulting sauce should be thick, rich, and noticeably tart from the acid present in the lemon. Adjust the seasoning with additional lemon juice, if necessary. Gently fold in the minced chives until distributed.

To Serve: Carefully slice the redfish fillets into 2-inch-wide portions, making a straight cut and being cautious not to tear the fish. Place the fish onto a serving platter and top each piece with a spoonful of warm Sweet Corn & Crab Sauce.

Working with Chili Peppers
When working with chilies of any specific heat level, it's recommended you wear a pair of gloves. It's not necessary, but it does allow for an element of control when dealing with the capsaicin present in the chili, allowing you to avoid spreading the active compound responsible for the heat in any chili to your work surface or parts of your body that would become instantly irritated from contact.

Suggested Pairing

Saison/Farmhouse Ale, Wallonia, Belgium

The origins for this unique style of beer hail from the Northern French speaking area of Belgium, where farmers would brew in the colder months for preservation and set the beer aside for consumption during the summer. Highly carbonated with fruity and spicy flavors, this ale was consumed by the seasonal workers (*saisonniers*) and provided them sustenance for their work day.

GRILLED SEA ROBIN WITH "FLAVORS OF PAELLA"

SERVES 8

ALTERNATIVE FISH: MONKFISH

Curated from an intent toward community, we celebrate what paella represents beyond its flavors and ingredients. Every day, we invest our passion and craft in our restaurants, engaging our guests and creating experiences that allow for families and friends to gather around a table to share in food and fellowship. Without having the capacity for a full, start-to-finish paella, and not being willing to adjust the cooking method of the traditional preparation, I often lean to this style of interpretation in the heat of summer. The flavors presented speak of a simple summer evening, gathered together with friends around an outdoor table, enjoying the crisp and hearty flavors inspired by the Spanish classic. Paella is an incredibly ingredient-driven dish. While we encourage creativity and resourcefulness, be thoughtful when making substitutions. That said, our modern-day knowledge and experience of paella is a bit different than its true origins. Ingredients and preparations vary by region and family custom. However you make it, do so with intention. Also, a quick note about saffron: I can't stress enough the importance of this ingredient in this preparation. The flavor of the saffron saturates the entire dish. The broth is very simple with the intention of acting as a delicate vehicle for the saffron notes.

SEA ROBIN

Sea robin, named after its elongated bird like fins, which are used to root out prey, is considered a trash species in the eyes of many, particularly recreational anglers who view them as a nuisance "bait stealer." Yet, the sea robin is highly prized and often used throughout Europe and France where it is known as gurnard and is the star ingredient in bouillabaisse. In New Zealand, the Bluefin sea robin finds its way to the dinner table. But in the United States, sea robins are typically discarded. Because sea robins share the same sandy habitat as flounders, particularly off the Atlantic Coast and in the Northeast, they are often caught incidentally by bottom fishermen targeting flounder or fluke. They've also been landed incidentally when trolling for mackerel. Coupled with their limited numbers, particularly in the Gulf of Maine, sea robins are simply not considered of potential commercial importance. Perhaps they should be?

The sea robin, like flounder, has a slightly firm texture with a sweet and mild flavor. Despite its head being big and bony, the tails of sea robin

CRISPY PAELLA RICE CAKES

⅓ cup Spanish olive oil + additional to finish

1 medium-size onion, peeled and minced

1 cup Calasparra or Bombe Rice

2 cups Chicken Stock (page 149)

1 cup Fumet (page 157)

8–12 saffron threads (or a good pinch)

Smoked sea salt, to finish

SAFFRON TOMATO BROTH
Makes about 2½ cups

3 tablespoons extra-virgin olive oil (Spanish preferred)

1 medium-size sweet onion, peeled and finely diced

Kosher salt, as needed

3 garlic cloves, smashed and peeled

1 teaspoon smoked paprika

½ cup dry white wine

4 fresh tomatoes (or 1 [28-ounce] can organic tomatoes crushed in juice)

12 saffron threads (or a good pinch)

ROASTED BABY SWEET PEPPERS

16 baby sweet peppers

Olive oil, as needed

GRILLED SEA ROBIN

2½ pounds sea robin fillets, cleaned and trimmed, skin removed

Spanish olive oil, as needed

Coarse sea salt, as needed

Smoked sea salt, as needed

2 cups cooked chorizo (see note on page 127)

Continued on page 126

TO MAKE THE CRISPY PAELLA RICE CAKES:

Heat a large sauté pan over medium heat for 2 or 3 minutes and add the olive oil. Allow the oil to heat for 30 to 45 seconds. Add the onion and sauté for 2 or 3 minutes or until soft and translucent. Add the rice and allow to toast in the oil for 45 to 60 seconds. Add the Chicken Stock and Fumet, along with the saffron threads, and bring to a boil. Stir the rice well and reduce the heat to very low, allowing for an incredibly gentle simmer. Cover and adjust the heat as necessary. Cook until the rice is tender, about 15 minutes. Check for doneness and adjust the cooking liquid if the rice appears dry and undercooked. Remove the lid and allow the pot to sit for 1 or 2 minutes to release some of the heat before handling. Pour the rice out onto an olive oil–greased baking sheet or baking pan (something with sides) and spread the rice evenly across the surface. Using slightly oiled hands, press the rice down firmly into the shape of the pan, achieving a thickness of at least 1 inch. Allow to cool fully, then cut the rice into 3-inch squares. Reserve.

TO MAKE THE SAFFRON TOMATO BROTH:

Heat a 4- or 6-quart saucepot over medium heat for 1 minute and add the olive oil. Allow the oil to heat for 30 seconds. Add the onion. Cook the onion over medium to high heat for 1 or 2 minutes, seasoning lightly with kosher salt. Add the garlic, careful not to let it burn. Add the smoked paprika and toast in the oil for 10 to 15 seconds, then add the wine. Allow the wine to come to boil, and reduce for 1 minute. Add the tomatoes and the saffron threads and bring to a hearty simmer. Cook the broth for 15 minutes, and allow to reduce by 20 percent. Remove from the heat and run through a fine mesh strainer. Do not push the solids through the strainer too aggressively. You should have a crisp, clean, light broth remaining.

TO MAKE THE ROASTED BABY SWEET PEPPERS:

Preheat the oven to 500°F. Coat the peppers well with olive oil and place on a baking sheet. Place in the oven or under the broiler and allow the peppers to char and blister without cooking too much and breaking down. Remove from the oven and set aside.

TO MAKE THE GRILLED SEA ROBIN:

Oil the sea robin fillets and season with the coarse sea salt. Note: Salt just prior to placing on the grill. Do not season in advance and allow the fish to sit. This will cause the salt to draw moisture from the fish, which also may cause the fish to stick to the grill. Grill the fish over raging hot coals until cooked through, achieving a blistery skin and charred exterior (for tips on grilling, see page xxxi).

Chorizo

While it's obvious that a traditional Spanish dish uses a traditional Spanish ingredient, we substitute the dried salami like Spanish chorizo with a fresh ground Mexican chorizo in the effort to celebrate our opportunity to use the best "stuff" we can find. The fresh sausage lends well to the textures and flavors of the final dish.

We have an incredibly dynamic Hispanic culture present in West Michigan, and we would do ourselves and our guests a disservice by making this preparation ourselves. It's one of the only products we purchase instead of processing in-house from whole, raw ingredients. Find a high-quality brand using well-sourced ingredients.

Next, heat a large sauté pan over medium heat. Add enough olive oil to coat the bottom of the pan. Allow the oil to heat for 25 to 30 seconds, and gently place the portioned Crispy Paella Rice Cakes into the hot oil. Sauté the cakes until brown and crispy, turning the rice cakes halfway through. Remove the rice cakes from the pan, transfer to paper towels, and sprinkle with smoked sea salt.

TO SERVE: In a large, shallow bowl, place a single Crispy Paella Rice Cake just off center on the dish. Place a small pile of 4 or 5 tablespoons of cooked chorizo over the cake, allowing to spill over one side of the rice. Place a sea robin fillet atop the rice and chorizo, and finish with 2 or 3 tablespoons of Saffron Tomato Broth. Garnish with a few Roasted Baby Sweet Peppers and drizzle with a bit of Spanish olive oil.

SUGGESTED PAIRING

Verdejo, Rueda, Spain

Grapes in this vast and warm region of northern Spain are harvested at night and cool-fermented to keep the grapes fresh and preserve flavor. Its flavors can vary, but most styles are blended with other varietals and display flavors of fresh citrus and lush herbs.

SKATE WING WITH LEMON & CAPERS

SERVES 4

ALTERNATIVE FISH: HADDOCK, FLOUNDER, SANDDABS, SOLE

The following dish is an homage to *grenobloise*, a classic dish featuring many of the components listed below. We celebrate intensity of flavor in the restaurant, as I often carry the personal philosophy of "If some is good, then more is better." The secret to the pan sauce is to add enough liquid (wine and lemon juice) and reduce heavily before adding the butter. The finished sauce, which will quickly become one of your favorites, is very intense, mouth-puckering at first, but immediately replaced with a rich and bold mouthfeel.

For more information on skate, see page 12.

CARAMELIZED LEMON SLICES
Neutral-flavored cooking oil

2 lemons, ends trimmed and sliced to ¼-inch thickness

PAN SAUCE
2 tablespoons cold butter, diced

3 tablespoons minced shallot

1 tablespoon minced garlic

¼ cup capers, well drained and rinsed

1 teaspoon red chili flakes

3 slices Caramelized Lemon

½ cup crisp dry white wine

½ cup freshly squeezed lemon juice

4 tablespoons cold butter, diced

2 tablespoons flat-leaf parsley, finely minced

Kosher salt, to taste

SKATE
4 (6-ounce) skate fillets, skin removed

Kosher salt, as needed

Granulated sugar, as needed

3 cups all-purpose flour

Cooking oil (e.g., vegetable, avocado, grapeseed)

TO MAKE THE CARAMELIZED LEMON SLICES:

Heat a medium sauté pan over moderate heat. Add the oil, simply enough to coat the bottom surface of the pan. Add the lemon slices, and allow the lemons to caramelize in the pan. Turn the slices, and finish caramelizing on the other side. Remove and allow to cool.

TO MAKE THE PAN SAUCE:

In a medium saucepan over medium-low heat, melt 2 tablespoons of the butter. Add the shallot and garlic and cook, stirring frequently, until shallot and garlic have started to soften, about 1 or 2 minutes. Add the capers, chili flakes, and Caramelized Lemon, and deglaze with the wine and lemon juice. Increase the heat slightly, and cook until the liquids have reduced *au sec*, or almost dry. Remove the pan from the heat and slowly add the remaining 4 tablespoons of butter in 1-tablespoon increments, whisking between each addition to ensure all butter is incorporated before adding the next tablespoon. Once all the butter is incorporated, add the parsley and season with salt to taste. The finished sauce should be thick and intense and very responsive to heat; a weak emulsion will be sensitive to breaking. Reserve and keep warm.

To make the Skate:

Pat the skate with a kitchen towel or paper towels. Season the skate (thoroughly but not excessively) with a 50/50 mixture of the kosher salt and granulated sugar. Place the skate into an appropriately sized dish and place in refrigerator for 1 hour.

Remove the skate from the refrigerator 30 minutes prior to cooking to allow the fish to come up in temperature. This will provide for even cooking. Pat the skate dry using a kitchen towel or paper towel. Excess moisture on the fish will cause it to stick to the pan and may cause the fish to steam instead of sear.

In a shallow baking dish, add the flour, and dip each skate wing in the flour, ensuring the fish is completely covered while shaking off excess flour.

Heat a large sauté pan over medium heat. Add the oil, and carefully place a skate wing in the pan. Cook until golden brown. Using a fish spatula, carefully turn the skate wing and cook on the opposite side until golden brown and fish is cooked through. Repeat with the remaining fillets.

To Serve: Spoon half the Pan Sauce onto the plate. Place a skate wing on top of the sauce, spooning additional sauce onto the skate, and garnish with Caramelized Lemon slices.

Suggested Pairing

Gruner Veltliner, Edna Valley, California, USA

Fans of Austrian Gruner Veltliner should take interest in the development of their beloved grape on the central coast of California. Each vintage achieves full ripeness and structure due to strong oceanic influences. Risk-taking winemakers have made international headlines with their take on these unconventional wines. Refreshingly crisp—driven with green apple, citrus, and mineral notes—these wines are an ideal pair for seafood.

SMOKED SKIPJACK TUNA TARTINE

SERVES 12

ALTERNATIVE FISH: ALBACORE, MAHI-MAHI, WAHOO

The following dish is one of many "toasts" that appear on our summer brunch menu. It was inspired after many mornings of preparing avocado toast and applying the composure of that creation as it changed from Sunday to Sunday to dial in the perfect "toast." The smoked skipjack tuna adds a heartiness that allows for this dish to be served as a first course or late lunch. As for the Fried Capers, these little guys are about as addictive as potato chips. Crunchy and salty, they add a perfect bite to any dish that involves capers as an ingredient. When fried properly, the capers will sprout open like little flowers. If well-fried, they will hold in a sealed container on the counter for up to one week.

For more information on skipjack tuna, see page 36.

SMOKED SKIPJACK TUNA
8 cups hot water

½ cup kosher salt

¼ cup granulated sugar

1 (3-pound) skipjack tuna fillet

12 slices (about 1¼-inch thick) brioche Pullman loaf

Garlic Shallot Mayonnaise (page 163), as needed

12 leaves Boston Bibb lettuce

Linnea's Sweet Pickles (page 162), for garnish

Pickled Mustard Seeds (page 167), for garnish

BOILED EGGS
Kosher salt, to season

1 tablespoon white distilled vinegar

9–12 farm-fresh pastured eggs

FRIED CAPERS
1 jar of salt-cured or brined capers

Frying oil, as needed

Fine salt, as needed

TO MAKE THE SMOKED SKIPJACK TUNA:

Place the hot water in a large bowl. Add the salt and sugar, and whisk until completely dissolved. Allow to cool to room temperature. Place the tuna fillet in a shallow baking dish and pour the cooled brine over the top. Allow to sit for 1 hour, then remove the fillet from the brine and place onto a baking tray lined with paper towels.

Next, transfer the fish onto a small wire rack rubbed lightly with oil and place into a smoker, ensuring the fish is located as far away from the heat source as possible. Gently smoke the fish at a consistent temperature of 225°F for 1¼ hours, or until the tuna has taken on a golden hue and the internal temperature of the fish is 175°F. Note: Be sure to bring the temperature of the smoker up to the cooking temperature of 225°F for a period of time before adding the fish to ensure a consistent temperature environment. Remove from smoker and reserve in refrigerator to cool.

If regularly purchasing eggs directly from a farm, you'll either want to age a few eggs in the back of the refrigerator for an extra week or ask the farmer for a few older cases for boiling. Fresh eggs are incredibly difficult to peel, as they haven't yet evaporated a small amount of their interior moisture content (which creates an air void between the egg and its shell). Eggs purchased from a grocery store are on average three or four weeks old when placed onto the shelf and are easily peeled. We recommend the aging method for a beautiful egg from the proper source.

To make the Boiled Eggs:

If you ask twelve different chefs what their preferred method of preparation for a "hard-boiled egg" is, you'll likely get twelve different responses. While there are many ways to "crack the code" to a much disputed and rarely achieved perfect result, this is my method:

Fill a 6-quart pot halfway with hot water and place over high heat. Season the water well with salt and a splash of the vinegar. Bring the water to a rolling boil, and very carefully lower the eggs into the water. Immediately cover the pot and turn off the heat. Set a timer for 10 minutes. When the timer goes off, remove 1 egg from the pot using a pair of tongs, and "smash" it on the countertop (or slice it with a knife like a civilized human) to evaluate the cooked state of the yolk. Assuming the yolk is a beautiful creamy yellow "medium" to your liking, immediately remove the eggs and place into an ice bath (half water, half ice) to shock the eggs and stop the cooking process. Once slightly cooled, peel the eggs and enjoy.

To make the Fried Capers:

Drain all the residual moisture from the capers. If using salt-cured capers, you will need a few rinses of clean water to remove the excess salt prior to use.

Place a 4-inch-tall medium pot over medium-high heat and fill with 1 inch of high-heat frying oil. Using a probe or candy thermometer, bring the temperature of the oil to 365°F.

Carefully add the capers to the hot oil. Stir with a spider or slotted spoon and allow the capers to fry for 45 seconds to 1 minute, or until the bubbles have subsided from the capers while frying. Scoop and drain the capers well from the frying oil and place onto paper towels. Season lightly with fine salt.

To Serve: Prepare the brioche by spreading a thin layer of the Garlic Shallot Mayonnaise onto the slices, coating both sides. Griddle the slices to a light, toasty golden brown and allow to cool. Spread 1½ tablespoons of Garlic Shallot Mayonnaise onto each toasted brioche slice and top with a leaf of Boston Bibb lettuce. Flake the chilled tuna onto each lettuce leaf, incorporating pieces of the Boiled Eggs and Linnea's Sweet Pickles as you go. Top with Pickled Mustard Seeds and Fried Capers.

SUGGESTED PAIRING

Lambrusco, Emilia-Romagna, Italy

Most Americans see Lambrusco as a sweet "soda pop" wine but traditional Lambrusco—the sparkling red from northeastern Italy—offers energetic, ripe berry fruit and can be dry or sweet. For pairing purposes, look for a nicely priced dry style that will provide ample value and versatile options.

WHOLE ROASTED SNAPPER WITH ARUGULA & SWEET PICKLED FENNEL

We take any opportunity available to roast whole fish right next to the fire in our wood-burning oven. We generally use carbon steel or cast iron when cooking next to the fire, although a basic baking sheet or roasting pan will work just as well. For a bit of added presentation value, feel free to flash the cooked fish under the broiler for just a moment prior to serving for a beautiful blister and additional caramelization.

NORTHERN RED SNAPPER

According to many experts, what you find at stores and restaurants isn't always what the label says. Case in point: the red snapper, arguably the most faked species and the poster child for improper seafood identification. Because the northern red snapper is similar in shape and appearance to other snappers, snappers like the mangrove snapper, mutton snapper, dog snapper, blackfin snapper, John snapper, Lane snapper, and Russell snapper may wind up with the label of red snapper by the time it hits the markets. The Pacific Sebastes rockfish is another species often mistaken for red snapper.

The northern red snapper, which is often found throughout the Gulf of Mexico and the Atlantic coast of the United States, is a prized fish by recreational anglers. Commercially, they are caught on multiple-hook gear, a system intended to land other commercially-viable species. Northern red snapper are also caught quite often by shrimp trawlers, making this snapper part of the shrimp fishermen's bycatch.

PICKLED FENNEL

3 heads fennel

1 yellow onion, peeled

3 cups white balsamic vinegar

1½ cups water

¾ cup granulated sugar

¾ cup kosher salt

2 tablespoons coriander seed, toasted and ground

2 tablespoons fennel seed, toasted and ground

SALSA VERDE*

2 garlic cloves, peeled and minced

1 medium-size shallot, peeled and minced

½ teaspoon red chili flakes

½ teaspoon fresh lemon zest

1 teaspoon Fresno chili (ribs, interior flesh and seeds removed), minced

¾ cup extra-virgin olive oil

¾ cup minced Italian parsley

1 tablespoon salt capers, rinsed well to remove excess salt

2 anchovy fillets, minced

3½ tablespoons freshly squeezed lemon juice

Coarse sea salt, as needed

ARUGULA SALAD

1 large bunch wild arugula or other hearty spicy green such as mustard or watercress

1 fresh whole fennel bulb, shaved thin and reserved in cold water, reserving the fronds

Extra-virgin olive oil, as needed

1 fresh lemon, halved

Coarse sea salt, as needed

RED SNAPPER

1 whole snapper (1 or 2 pounds), scaled and cleaned

Extra-virgin olive oil, as needed

Coarse sea salt, as needed

*This recipe makes more than what will be required for the dish, but is a terrific item to have stored in the refrigerator to use in a pinch. The sweetness and acidity pair incredibly well with many varieties and preparations of seafood.

Continued on page 138

TO MAKE THE PICKLED FENNEL:

Thinly slice the fennel and onion, and transfer to a large container. Meanwhile, in a saucepot, add the vinegar, water, sugar, salt, coriander, and fennel seeds. Bring to a boil. Remove from heat, and pour the liquid over the fennel and onion. Let sit for at least 12 hours.

TO MAKE THE SALSA VERDE:

In a non reactive bowl, combine all the ingredients, except the lemon juice. Allow the mixture to sit for 1 hour. Just prior to serving, add the lemon juice and combine well.

TO MAKE THE ARUGULA SALAD:

Clean the arugula well, dry, and place into a medium-size mixing bowl. Remove the fennel from the water, tamp dry, and add to the arugula along with the fronds. Dress the mixture very lightly with the olive oil, add an equal amount of lemon juice (squeezed fresh), and season with the coarse salt.

TO MAKE THE RED SNAPPER:

Preheat the oven to 425°F. Place the fish on a cutting board and trim off the fins and the tail using poultry shears or utility kitchen shears (this is to avoid burning during the cooking process). Using a very sharp knife, cut 3 or 4 slashes (about ¼-inch deep) into the flesh of the fish every 1½ inches. Turn the fish over and repeat the same cuts on the other side.

Coat both sides of the fish well with the olive oil. Place the fish onto a roasting sheet and season well with the sea salt.

Place the fish on the center rack of the oven and roast for 15 to 18 minutes, or until the flesh is firm and the skin has taken on a toasted, caramelized appearance.

TO SERVE: Place the whole fish onto a large serving platter. Spoon an abundant amount of the Salsa Verde over the fish and spread across the surface using the back of the spoon. Place the Arugula Salad alongside the fish and garnish with the Pickled Fennel (ensuring that it has been drained well of its pickling liquid prior to plating).

SUGGESTED PAIRING

Chardonnay, Lake Michigan Shore, Michigan USA

Located in southwestern Michigan, the Lake Michigan Shore AVA (American Viticulture Area) is home to many cool climate varietals. The region's proximity to Lake Michigan provides a unique micro-climate, perfect for growing many of the noble *vinifera* grape varieties from which the world's greatest wines are made. Chardonnay from this coastal Great Lakes region displays flavors of sweet yellow apple, ripe pear, and a lingering dry finish.

RECIPE FOUNDATIONS

BRANDADE

This rustic and chunky "mash" is fantastic with smoked fish and incredible when spread on a slice of crusty bread and placed under the broiler until golden brown or simply served cold with crackers. Although salt-preserved cod is traditional to the origins of this dish, it's delicious with slow-poached monkfish and roasted flounder and provides a great opportunity to use leftover portions of a previous seafood preparation.

1½ pounds Smoked Mullet (page 60)

1 pound small potatoes (German butterball, Klondike, fingerling)

½ cup oil from Confit Garlic & Shallot with Oil (page 151)

6 Confit Garlic cloves, from Confit Garlic and Shallot Oil recipe (page 151)

¼ teaspoon red chili flakes

½ cup heavy cream

Sea salt, to taste

Remove and flake the flesh of the Smoked Mullet and discard the skin. Set aside.

Boil the potatoes, reducing the heat slightly once boiling temperature has been reached, as to not damage or break the potatoes. Allow to simmer gently until tender, about 20 minutes after boiling. Remove from heat and drain the water, reserving the potatoes in the cooking pot. Add the Smoked Mullet, Confit Garlic & Shallot Oil, Confit Garlic cloves, red chili flakes, and the heavy cream. Season with salt. Be careful not to oversalt or overmix. Adjust the consistency with additional cream or Confit Garlic & Shallot Oil if desired.

BUTTERMILK VINAIGRETTE

Makes 1½ cups

Double or triple this recipe before you step foot in the kitchen. It's the embodiment of summertime and delicious with anything that would benefit from a garden full of herbs.

8 ounces sour cream

¼ cup buttermilk

¼ teaspoon minced thyme

1¼ teaspoons minced chives

1¼ teaspoons minced dill

¾ teaspoon minced basil

¾ teaspoon minced garlic

½ teaspoon dill pollen

Fine sea salt, to taste

In a large mixing bowl, combine the sour cream, buttermilk, thyme, chives, dill, basil, garlic, and dill pollen. Season to taste with fine sea salt.

CAPER ANCHOVY VINAIGRETTE

3 tablespoons capers, removed from brine and rinsed

½ cup Nicoise olives, pits removed

4 white anchovies, soaked in milk for 10 minutes

½ cup Reserved Poaching Oil (page 37), may be substituted with Extra Virgin Olive Oil

Fresh squeezed lemon juice

In a mixing bowl, combine the capers, olives, anchovies, Reserved Poaching Oil, and lemon juice. Whisk or purée to a fine consistency.

CARAMELIZED LEEKS

1 pound salted butter

10–12 medium leeks, washed well and diced

Kosher salt, as needed

In a large pot, melt the butter and add the leeks. Sprinkle with some salt to encourage moisture removal from the leeks. Stir the leeks often to ensure even cooking as the moisture continues to evaporate. Cook for 15 to 20 minutes. Once the leeks have begun to weep and a bulk of their moisture has been drawn out and evaporated, the leeks will take on slight caramelization. Lower the heat, and cook for an additional 30 to 40 minutes over low heat, stirring often. Once the leeks have cooked down significantly and taken on a deep golden caramelization, remove from the heat and allow to cool. Reserve in the refrigerator until ready to use.

CELERY VERDE

2 cups celery, small dice

1 cup celery leaf, minced

½ cup tarragon, minced

1 cup capers, chopped

½ teaspoon red chili flakes

1 garlic clove, peeled and minced

1½ cups fresh flat-leaf parsley, minced

3 tablespoons Dijon mustard

2 cups olive oil

Kosher salt, to taste

In a small mixing bowl, combine the celery, celery leaf, tarragon, capers, chili flakes, garlic, parsley, mustard, and olive oil. Season with salt to taste.

CELERY VINAIGRETTE

MAKES ABOUT 1 CUP

This bright and vibrant sauce is best left to blend immediately prior to serving.

4 stalks celery, chopped

½ cup flat-leaf parsley

3 garlic cloves, peeled

⅛ cup chives, chopped

½ medium shallot, peeled

3 tablespoons white wine vinegar, divided

½ cup olive oil, divided

Kosher salt, to taste

Into the jar of a blender, add the celery, parsley, garlic, chives, shallot, 2 tablespoons of the vinegar, and one-quarter of the olive oil. Blend until smooth, adjusting the consistency as necessary using the remaining olive oil. Season well with salt and balance the acidity to your liking with the additional vinegar.

CHARRED LEEKS

6 leeks, leaves and root removed, washed well

Extra-virgin olive oil, as needed

Coat the leek stalks well with oil. Preheat an outdoor grill on high. Place the leeks over the heat and move consistently until well-charred and blistered (for tips on grilling, see page xxxi). Remove the leeks from the grill and wrap in a foil pouch, returning to the grill in an indirect heating spot or grill temperature reduced to low. Cook for 10 to 12 minutes or until leeks are tender throughout. Cool the leeks thoroughly. Reserve until ready to use.

Note: If using a stovetop: Coat the leek stalks well with oil. Heat a large sauté pan over medium heat and add 1 to 2 tablespoons of oil, then add the leeks. Cook the leeks in the oil, turning them frequently to achieve a char and blister on the outer leaves. Remove from the oil and allow to cool slightly. Wrap the leeks in foil and place into a preheated 300°F oven for 25 minutes or until tender throughout. Chill the cooked leeks thoroughly. Reserve until ready to use.

CHICKEN STOCK

MAKES ABOUT 4 QUARTS

While ultimately a simple process, there's nothing more satisfying than a pot of stock started in the morning, yielding to the foundation of a great dinner.

5 pounds chicken bones, rinsed well

2 large onions, peeled and medium dice

3 medium-size carrots, peeled and medium dice

4 stalks celery

4 sprigs fresh thyme

1 tablespoon toasted black peppercorns

2 fresh bay leaves

4 sprigs flat-leaf parsley

In a large stockpot, add the bones and cover by 2 inches of cold water. Bring the water to an almost boil over medium-high heat. Skim off the foam impurities with a ladle and discard. Reduce the heat so the stock is at a slow simmer. Simmer for about 1 hour, skimming as needed. Add the onions, carrots, celery, thyme, peppercorns, bay leaves, and parsley. Simmer for an additional 45 minutes. Remove from heat, strain, and cool until needed.

CONFIT FINGERLING POTATOES

16 small fingerling potatoes, split lengthwise

2 quarts rendered pork fat, bacon fat, or extra-virgin olive oil

Preheat the oven to 325°F.

Place the potatoes into a small pan and cover well with the fat, ensuring the potatoes are fully submerged. Cover the pan with foil and place in the oven. Cook for 35 to 40 minutes or until potatoes are tender while ensuring the potatoes do not take on color or caramelization. Remove from the oven and allow to cool. Remove the potatoes from the cooking fat and allow to drain well. Reserve in the refrigerator until ready to use.

CONFIT GARLIC & SHALLOT

(WITH OIL)

16 garlic cloves, peeled

12 peeled shallots, ends trimmed

Extra-virgin olive oil, or neutral-flavored oil (e.g., grapeseed or canola)

Preheat the oven to 325°F.

Place the garlic and shallots in a suitably sized ovenproof dish. Cover the garlic and shallots with the oil. Cover the dish with foil and place in the oven. Cook for 1½ to 2 hours, or until the shallots are very tender. Remove from oven and allow to cool. Store in the refrigerator until ready to use.

CONFIT PORK BELLY

5 pounds fresh heritage breed pasture-raised pork belly

8 ounces kosher salt

4 ounces granulated sugar

½ teaspoon sodium nitrate (pink curing salt)

1 teaspoon toasted crushed black peppercorn

1 teaspoon red chili flakes

1 teaspoon toasted crushed coriander seed

1 teaspoon toasted crushed fennel seed

1 teaspoon toasted crushed cumin seed

4 pounds rendered pork fat or lard

Place the pork belly in a small container. Season well with the spices reserving 2 tablespoons. Once coated, place the pork belly into a large ziptop bag and add an additional 2 tablespoons of the spice mixture to the pork. Remove all the air from the bag and seal. Place in the refrigerator. Cure the pork belly for 4 to 5 days, turning the bag every day to redistribute the cure. On the last day, remove the pork from the bag and rinse well with cold water. Pat dry and prepare for the Confit.

Preheat the oven to 315°F.

Melt the pork fat slowly in a medium saucepan. Place the pork belly into an ovenproof container that is at least 5 inches taller than the height of the belly. Carefully pour the melted fat over the pork, ensuring the belly is submerged. Cover the container with foil and place in the oven. Allow to cook for 3 to 4 hours, or until pork, when penetrated with a fork, offers very slight resistance, but does not fall apart. Remove from heat and allow to cool. Place the pork belly, still submerged in fat, into the refrigerator overnight. The following day, peel away the soft cooking fat and clean the pork belly. The pork belly can be portioned and used or wrapped well and reserved in the refrigerator or freezer.

COUNTRY DREDGE

1½ cups all-purpose flour

2 teaspoons dried thyme, finely ground

1 tablespoon + 1 teaspoon smoked paprika

1 tablespoon + 1 teaspoon black pepper, finely ground

2 teaspoons onion powder

2 teaspoons garlic powder

1 cup cornstarch

In a small bowl, whisk the flour, thyme, paprika, pepper, onion powder, garlic powder, and cornstarch together until combined. Reserve until ready to use.

COURT BOUILLON

Makes about 6 quarts

This classical version of "short stock" is a quick way to facilitate flavor when poaching or resting various types of seafood.

1½ gallons water

2 medium-size onions, peeled and chopped

1 medium-size leek, chopped

2 medium-size carrots, chopped

3 stalks celery, chopped

4 sprigs flat-leaf parsley, chopped

3 sprigs fresh thyme

1 tablespoon black peppercorns, toasted

2 sprigs fresh oregano

2 fresh bay leaves (or dried)

3 tablespoons kosher salt

3 cups white wine vinegar

In a large stock pot, add the water, onions, leek, carrots, celery, parsley, thyme, peppercorns, oregano, bay leaves, salt, and vinegar. Bring to a boil, reduce the heat, and simmer for 30 minutes. Run through a fine mesh strainer and reserve.

DILL CREAM

Makes 2 cups

2 cups sour cream

¼ cup buttermilk

3 tablespoons fresh dill, minced

⅛ teaspoon dill pollen, crushed between fingers

In a small mixing bowl, add the sour cream, buttermilk, dill, and dill pollen. Be sure to crush the dill pollen between your fingertips as you add it to the mixture. Stir to combine.

DILL VINAIGRETTE

2 cups sour cream

3 tablespoons buttermilk

1 tablespoon dill pollen

2 tablespoons minced fresh dill

1 tablespoon white distilled vinegar

Kosher salt, to taste

In a medium-size mixing bowl, combine the sour cream, buttermilk, dill pollen, dill, and vinegar. Season to taste with salt.

DILL PICKLES

While we take every opportunity to utilize lacto-fermentation in our preservation needs at the restaurant, the intensity of our summer season demands a faster alternative that's just as delicious.

1 quart water

6 tablespoons kosher salt

4 tablespoons sugar

1½ teaspoons peppercorns, toasted

1 tablespoon coriander seed, toasted

¾ teaspoon red chili flakes

½ cup white vinegar

20 cloves garlic, smashed and peeled

½ bunch fresh dill

1 pound pickling cucumbers

In a 4-quart saucepot, bring the water to a boil. Add the salt, sugar, peppercorns, coriander, chili flakes, vinegar, and garlic. Whisk until the salt and sugar have completely dissolved. Remove the pot from the heat and allow to cool to room temperature. Add the fresh dill and pour the brine over the cucumbers. Place into sterilized mason jars and process or place in an appropriately sized container. Transfer to the refrigerator and let sit at least 1 week before serving.

FRESH BREADCRUMBS

This may easily be interpreted as an unnecessary project, but freshly ground breadcrumbs make a world of difference in a multitude of preparations. The texture and capacity for use in a panade or as a breading medium or thickening agent is far superior than any store-bought option. It also has the added benefit of being an excellent resource for utilizing what may otherwise become waste.

For fresh coarse breadcrumbs: Place stale bread (or slice fresh bread, and allow to sit uncovered overnight) into the bowl of a food processor and pulse until a consistent crumb. Transfer to a ziptop bag and store in the freezer.

For finer breadcrumbs: Allow the processed fresh breadcrumbs to lay on a baking sheet in an even layer overnight or until well dried. Ensure the crumbs are not packed too closely as you dry them, as they will lose the necessary opportunity to release moisture, and could become moldy. Once thoroughly dried, place the crumbs back into the bowl of a food processor, and process until the desired texture is achieved.

FUMET

4 to 5 pounds fish bones (preferably a light white-fleshed fish such as flounder, snapper, or sole—heads recommended, but ensure gills and eyes are removed)

4 tablespoons vegetable oil or extra-virgin olive oil

2 medium sweet onions, sliced

½ small fennel bulb, sliced thin

12 small leeks, cleaned well and sliced thin into rings

1 teaspoon kosher salt

2 cups dry white wine

2 sprigs fresh flat-leaf parsley

6 fresh laurel leaves (or 2 dried bay leaves)

12 whole black peppercorns

6 cups water

To make the Fumet:

Place the fish bones in a large, suitable container. Cover the bones with cold water, drain the water, and cover again with fresh water. Allow the bones to sit in the cold water for 30 minutes, and repeat this soak-and-rinse step one additional time, allowing for bones to sit for a final 30 minutes. Drain the bones.

In a large, heavy-bottomed pot over moderate heat, heat the oil and add the onions, fennel, and leeks. Sweat the vegetables for 1 to 2 minutes, ensuring they do not take on any color or caramelization. Sprinkle with the kosher salt (Note: this salting step is not for seasoning, but instead to draw moisture from the vegetables and intensify their flavor as they cook), and allow to cook for an additional 2 to 3 minutes or until tender and translucent. Add the fish bones/heads and cook until the flesh remaining on the bones becomes white and opaque. Add the wine and allow to cook for 1 to 2 minutes to reduce the wine slightly. Add the parsley sprigs, laurel leaves (or bay leaves), peppercorns, and water. Bring to a boil, and reduce the heat just slightly so the boil is present but not too aggressive. Cook the Fumet for 15 minutes. Using a ladle, skim off any foam and impurities that rise to the surface. Remove from heat and strain the Fumet through a fine sieve, chinois, coffee filter, or cheesecloth. Allow to cool, and then reserve in the refrigerator until ready to use.

GARLIC BREAD

Source a high-quality, fresh artisan bread made from quality flour. We recommend sourdough, a simple French loaf, or substitute your favorite style of hearth bread.

1 cup Spicy Garlic Butter (page 172) or Confit Garlic & Shallot Oil (page 151)

4 slices (½- to ¾-inch thick) sourdough baguette or loaf, cut on the bias

Coarse sea salt or flake salt, as needed

Preheat the oven to 425°F.

Melt the butter gently and apply liberally to both sides of the bread. Place on a large baking sheet. Sprinkle aggressively with salt. Bake in the oven quickly, 5 or 6 minutes, or until the bottom crust is toasted and the top edges of the bread have begun to brown. The garlic bread should be crunchy on the exterior and retain its soft interior.

HORSERADISH MAYONNAISE

Makes 1 quart

6 tablespoons lemon juice

¼ cup white wine vinegar

6 tablespoons grated horseradish

3 egg yolks

1 tablespoon Dijon mustard

1 tablespoon lemon zest

1½ cups vegetable oil

1½ cups olive oil

Kosher salt, to taste

In a small mixing bowl, combine the lemon juice and vinegar, and set aside.

Place the horseradish, egg yolks, mustard, and lemon zest into the bowl of a food processor. Purée until smooth. With the food processor running, slowly add the oils in a thin stream. As the mixture thickens, add the lemon juice/vinegar slowly to thin. Season to taste with kosher salt.

LINNEA'S SWEET PICKLES

MAKES 3 QUARTS

This Bread & Butter pickled cucumber recipe was simply referred to as "pickles" growing up, as it was the only pickled preparation found in the family refrigerator. Make these sweet pickles and use them anytime you would normally reach for a jar of grocery store "sweet relish." Be sure to source cucumbers from the local farms when the pickling varieties are at their prime. While some elements of this recipe conflict with how we would naturally approach the preparation in the restaurant kitchen, one does not question Grandma's recipe.

- 15–20 small/medium-size cucumbers, washed and thinly sliced
- 5 cups onions, peeled and sliced into thin rings
- 2 sweet peppers (red and green), very small dice
- ½ cup kosher salt
- ½ cup distilled water
- 2½ cups high-quality apple cider vinegar
- 2½ cups distilled water
- 3 cups granulated sugar
- 2 tablespoons whole mustard seeds
- 1 teaspoon ground turmeric
- ½ teaspoon fresh ground clove

In a large container, combine the cucumbers, onions, sweet peppers, salt, and water and allow to sit overnight. Next, in a non reactive saucepot over medium-high heat, add the vinegar, water, sugar, mustard seeds, turmeric, and clove. Bring to a boil. Drain the initial cucumber preparation, and add to the vinegar mixture on the stove. Allow the cucumbers to marinate in the vinegar mixture over heat for 3 minutes. Remove from heat and transfer to a container to cool or pack into jars and process.

MALT VINEGAR MAYONNAISE

MAKES 2 CUPS

This recipe eliminates the intensity of the Confit Garlic & Shallot used as a foundation for derivative mayonnaise preparations we typically create so that the flavor is focused on the malt.

In a pinch, season up our "basic" mayonnaise with malt vinegar powder or a few dashes of your favorite brand.

- 2 egg yolks
- 1 tablespoon Dijon mustard
- 4 tablespoons malt vinegar, divided
- 1 cup oil, such as grapeseed or vegetable oil
- Water, as needed
- 2 tablespoons fresh-squeezed lemon juice
- Kosher salt, as needed

Place the egg yolks and mustard, along with half of the malt vinegar, into the bottom of a speed-adjustable blender. Place the top on the blender and start on low speed to incorporate the emulsifiers. Increase the speed of the blender to low/medium and remove the small access plug from the top of the blender. Begin slowly adding the oil into the blender. Once half of the oil has been added and the mixture has thickened significantly, add the remaining malt vinegar to thin the emulsion slightly. Repeat the process of drizzling the oil into the blender. If the mixture at any time becomes so thick that it stops moving through the blade in a vortex, thin the mixture slightly with a splash of water and proceed to incorporate the remaining oil. Season and balance the mayonnaise with the lemon juice and salt to your taste.

Note: When using a blender to create this preparation, be mindful that the movement of the blade through the ingredients will create friction, which will translate to heat. If the blender is left running excessively through the preparation, the excess heat generated may cause the mayonnaise to break. If this happens, remove the entire contents of the blender and start again with the yolks and mustard, slowly drizzling the broken, watery mayonnaise into the blender in the same method as stated above.

MAYONNAISE WITH CONFIT GARLIC & SHALLOT

MAKES 3 CUPS–1 QUART (DEPENDING ON PREFERRED THICKNESS)

This recipe is our "basic" mayonnaise and as foundational as it gets when it comes to mayo in our world. I could write page after page of ways to use the Confit Garlic & Shallot, which is the base for our emulsion. The Confit Garlic & Shallot preparation always results in more oil than is necessary for the production of the mayonnaise, yet I guarantee you'll never question an opportunity to use it. Make this recipe once, and you'll forever scoff at the condiment shelf of the grocery. Mayonnaise is one of the most gratifying projects to prepare at home. Here, we're utilizing a blender to create our emulsion, but it's highly encouraged that you attempt the same process using a mixing bowl and a fine wire whisk.

2 egg yolks

1 tablespoon Dijon mustard

8 Confit Garlic cloves (page 151)

3 small to medium-size Confit Shallots (page 151)

½ teaspoon lemon zest

3 tablespoons fresh-squeezed lemon juice

2½ cups Confit Garlic & Shallot oil (page 151)

Water, as needed

Fine sea salt, as needed

Place the egg yolks and the Dijon, along with the Confit Garlic and Shallots, into the bottom of a speed-adjustable blender. Place the top on the blender and start on low speed. Increase the speed of the blender to low/medium and remove the small access plug from the top of the blender. Add the lemon zest and 1 tablespoon of the lemon juice, and then proceed with the Confit Garlic & Shallot. Once half of the oil has been added and the mixture has thickened significantly, add another tablespoon of the remaining lemon juice. Your indication to thin the mixture using the lemon juice (or water) is when the "vortex" (or tornado, the constant swirling feed of the mixture moving from the top of the jar down into the blade) begins to struggle, stiffen, or stop; at this point, thin the emulsion slightly. Repeat the process of drizzling the oil into the blender in the same manner as described above. Season the mayonnaise with the lemon juice and salt to your taste.

Notes: If preparing a larger batch of mayonnaise, or the recipe exceeds the capacity of your equipment, remove 75 percent of the product from the blender jar when it is at a thick and stiff point in the back and forth process of the emulsion, using the remaining 25 percent of existing mayonnaise as your base to continue the addition of oil. If using this method, be sure to season and mix the final quantity together.

When using a blender to create this preparation, be mindful that the movement of the blade through the ingredients will create friction, which will translate to heat. If the blender is left running excessively through the preparation, the excess heat generated may very likely cause the mayonnaise to break. If this happens, remove the entire contents of the blender, and start again with the yolks and mustard, slowly drizzling the broken, watery mayonnaise into the blender in the same method as noted above.

OLIVE TAPENADE

Makes 1½ quarts

3½ ounces peeled garlic cloves

28 ounces Kalamata olives, drained

3 ounces capers, drained

1 tablespoon oregano leaves

Zest of 4 lemons

2 cups olive oil

In a food processor, add the garlic, olives, capers, oregano, and lemon zest. Purée while slowly adding the olive oil until combined.

PICKLED BEETS

Makes 8 pounds

8 pounds beets (if using various colors, keep separate)

Kosher salt

2 cups water

4 cups white wine vinegar

¼ cup salt

¼ cup sugar

1 bay leaf

1½ teaspoons cardamom seeds

1½ teaspoons anise seed

1 tablespoon mustard seed

2 tablespoons coriander seed, toasted

1½ teaspoons juniper berries

1 tablespoon black peppercorns, toasted

Preheat the oven to 400°F.

Peel the beets with a vegetable peeler. Place on a baking dish, and season well with kosher salt. Cover with aluminum foil and roast in the oven until tender (cooking time will vary depending on the size of the beets; small beets should take about 45 minutes while larger beets between 45 minutes and 1½ hours). When roasted, remove from oven and allow to cool. Then cut into ½ -inch-thick slices and place in a large bowl.

In a saucepot, add the water, vinegar, salt, sugar, bay leaf, cardamom, anise, mustard, and coriander seeds, juniper berries, and peppercorns. Bring to a boil. Cool to room temperature and pour over the beets. Refrigerate the beets at least 1 day before serving.

PICKLED GREEN TOMATOES

4 pounds green tomatoes (about 6 medium-size tomatoes), washed well

1 quart water

1 quart apple cider vinegar

8 teaspoons kosher salt

4 teaspoons sugar

2 teaspoons whole cumin seed, toasted

1 teaspoon whole coriander seed

2 jalapeño peppers, split lengthwise

Gently prick the tomatoes all over with a toothpick and place in an appropriately sized container. In a non reactive saucepot, add the water, vinegar, salt, sugar, cumin, coriander, and jalapeños. Bring to a boil. Remove from the heat and strain. Allow the liquid to cool for about 15 minutes. Pour the cooled liquid over the green tomatoes, ensuring they are fully submerged. Allow to sit for 1 week. Note: To speed up the brine time, dice or slice the tomatoes prior to brining.

PICKLED MUSTARD SEEDS

Makes 2 cups

We absolutely love the subtle mustard flavor presented in this seafood accompaniment. The mustard seeds add a very pleasant texture to any dish while also offering a fantastic visual appeal. Note that the mustard seeds will tend to fall to the bottom of the pot and stick as they progress through the process of rinsing/boiling. Be sure to stir well during the cooking process.

1 quart water

1 cup yellow mustard seeds

2 cups white balsamic vinegar

4 teaspoons salt

2 teaspoons sugar

In a saucepot over medium heat, bring the water to a boil. Add the mustard seeds and cook for 30 seconds, stirring often. Strain and rinse well in cold water. Repeat this process of boiling and rinsing the mustards seeds 5 times (this is to remove any bitter tannins present). Transfer the mustard seeds to a bowl.

Next, add the vinegar, salt, and sugar to the saucepot over medium heat and bring to a boil. Remove from heat and pour the brine over the mustard seeds. Allow to cool to room temperature. When cool, cover and leave out at room temperature overnight.

PRESERVED & CARAMELIZED LEMON

Makes ¾ cup

We often use this preparation to benefit from the incredible intensity found in this reduction. More often, we use it as a seasoning and flavoring agent for derivative recipes. It's an incredible option to have available when seeking out a unique citrus note when creating a dish.

In a wide, heavy-bottomed pot, place the preserved lemons, making sure to scrape all the juices and extra seasoning from the curing process. Place over low heat and cook, stirring often. The lemons will first break down and release all their liquids, and once the liquids have reduced, they will slowly caramelize. You will want to cook this mixture very slowly, until a deep brown caramelization occurs, which can take several hours. Once finished, purée well and strain.

PRESERVED LEMON

In Michigan, we have easy access to many heirloom varieties of citrus when they're at the peak of their season and available to us in the winter. We take every opportunity to preserve these special lemons when we're easily prompted to gravitate toward citrus in the summer. This recipe can be applied to other citrus, as well.

10 whole lemons

1 cup granulated sugar

1 cup kosher salt

Wash the lemons and slice into ½-inch thick slices. In a mixing bowl, combine the sugar and salt. In a non reactive, 9-inch square cake pan (glass or stainless steel) or other similar container, place a single layer of lemon slices. Sprinkle well with the seasoned mixture. Continue until all the lemon slices are covered. Wrap or cover and allow to sit at room temperature for 3 days. After 3 days, place into the refrigerator. Wait a minimum of 3 additional days before using.

You can also caramelize the preserved lemons for an intense seasoning. See next recipe.

ROASTED APPLES

We recommend using a firm, crisp, tart apple such as honey crisp. We love using honey crisp apples in the restaurant because of their ability to be exposed to air and not turn brown or oxidize. This allows us to produce portions of cut apples at a time without the necessity of an acid bath, which will ultimately alter the flavor of the apple to some degree.

2 honey crisp apples, cored and quartered

Walnut oil, as needed

Preheat the oven to 425°F.

Place the apple quarters onto a walnut-oiled baking sheet. Do not season. Roast the apples for 12 to 14 minutes, or until lightly caramelized and slightly softened. Remove from the oven and allow to cool.

ROASTED PEPPER MUSTARD

Makes 4 cups

We prepare large amounts of this mustard at the end of the growing season to utilize an excessive amount of hot pepper varieties that grow in our garden at the restaurant. The relative heat of the final result can be easily altered by choosing milder peppers. Stored in the refrigerator, you can enjoy this condiment all winter.

16 medium-size moderate heat level peppers, such as banana or Hungarian hot

1 medium sweet onion, peeled and diced

8 garlic cloves, peeled

2 cups white distilled vinegar

1½ cups classic yellow mustard

1 tablespoon dry mustard powder

¾ cup honey

Kosher salt, to taste

In a medium-size saucepot, combine the peppers, onion, garlic, vinegar, mustard, dry mustard, and honey. Slowly heat to a simmer. Cook for 20 to 25 minutes, stirring often. Once the peppers and onion are tender, and the mixture has reduced slightly, remove from heat and allow to cool. Once mixture has cooled, transfer to a blender, and purée until smooth. If a finer final texture is desired, push through a fine strainer. Season with salt to taste, and adjust with additional vinegar or honey to achieve your desired sweetness/acidity.

SPICY GARLIC BUTTER

MAKES 2¼ CUPS

1 pound butter, divided

1 head garlic, smashed and peeled

½–1 tablespoon red chili flakes, depending on desired heat

2 tablespoons finely minced flat-leaf parsley, for garnish

In a medium saucepot over low heat, slowly melt half the butter. Do not allow the temperature of the butter to get too high. If the butter gets too hot, the milk solids present will caramelize, altering the fresh, whole butter flavor that is intended. Add the garlic cloves and let infuse for 2 or 3 minutes before adding the chili flakes. Remove the mixture from the heat and allow to cool for 10 minutes. Add the remaining butter to the cooled mixture, a little at a time, until fully incorporated. Stir in the parsley to the soft butter mixture. Note: If the butter is too warm when the parsley is added, the parsley, along with the garlic and chili flakes, will sink to the bottom of the container and eliminate the opportunity for even usage once stored.

SWEET CORN STOCK

MAKES 3 TO 4 CUPS

One of the early jobs given to Lalo, an amazing and hardworking individual at Salt of the Earth, was the task of processing mountains of sweet corn by removing the husks, cleaning the remaining silk, removing the kernels from the cobs, then labeling and storing the corn for further preparation. It should be noted that Lalo didn't speak much English and a great deal of specifics were often lost in transition. Upon entering the walk-in cooler that day, I discovered the cleaned corn cobs (ready for stock production) in a tightly covered container with the label "Bones Corn." Corn cobs have been known as "Bones Corn" in my kitchen ever since.

4 corn cobs, kernels removed

3 fresh laurel leaves, or 1 dried bay leaf

1 tablespoon whole black peppercorns, toasted

1 tablespoon whole coriander seeds, toasted

4 garlic cloves, smashed and peeled

1 shallot, peeled and sliced into ⅛-inch rings

1½–2 quarts cold water

Place the corn cobs (or more if available or desired) into a pot large enough to hold them. Add the laurel leaves, peppercorns, coriander, garlic, and shallot. Cover well with the water. Bring the pot almost to a boil, and allow to gently simmer for 25 to 30 minutes, skimming off any impurities that foam and rise to the surface during cooking. Remove the pot from the heat and run through a fine mesh strainer, chinois, or cheesecloth. Place the strained stock back into the pot and return to the heat. Bring to a boil and reduce by half. Reserve.

SWEET PICKLED APPLES

Essentially pickled, this fantastic preparation is the perfect way to preserve the fall harvest and allow for a quick and easy addition to any dish that requires a bit of sweetness as well as acidity.

4 apples (such as honey crisp), cored and quartered

1 cup apple cider

1 cup white distilled vinegar

1 tablespoon toasted coriander seed

1 teaspoon toasted anise seed

1 teaspoon toasted Szechuan peppercorns

¼ cup honey

2 tablespoon brown sugar

Place the apples in a large bowl. In a medium-size saucepot over medium heat, add the cider, vinegar, coriander and anise seeds, peppercorns, honey, and brown sugar. Whisk to dissolve the sugar and honey. Remove from heat, pour the hot brine over the apples, and refrigerate at least 6 hours before serving.

SWEET PICKLED PEARL ONIONS

Makes 5 pounds

5 pounds peeled pearl onions

3 cups white balsamic vinegar

2 cups water

¾ cup granulated sugar

½ cup kosher salt

2 tablespoons whole coriander seed, toasted

1 tablespoon anise seed, toasted

2 tablespoons juniper berries

1 teaspoon black peppercorns, toasted

Place the onions in a large bowl.

In a medium non reactive pot over medium heat, add the vinegar, water, sugar, salt, coriander and anise seeds, juniper berries, and black peppercorns. Bring to a boil, remove from heat, and let cool. Strain the liquid over the pearl onions and allow the onions to steep for at least 6 hours prior to using. If stored in a sealed glass container in the refrigerator, the onions should last for 3 to 6 months.

174   Sea Robins, Triggerfish & Other Overlooked Seafood

RESOURCES

Of course, this book could not be complete without mentioning some of the superior products Chef Matthew uses every day at his award-winning restaurants.

Whether you're a professional chef or a weekend griller, the following companies feature high-quality products to help you when it comes to preparing and serving delicious seafood for your family and friends.

Anova Culinary

Thermal Immersion Circulators

Anova was founded in 2013 and motivated by two equally important ideas: (1) Use science and technology to change the way people cook; and (2) the devices should be accessible to everyone. Since that time, Anova focused relentlessly on making the best precision cooking devices in the world and selling them at an affordable price-point. Visit them at www.anovaculinary.com.

BLiS

The BLiS Gourmet line consists of bourbon barrel–aged sauces and wild-caught domestic roes handcrafted in Grand Rapids, Michigan. BLiS barrel ages everything from locally sourced maple syrup to hot sauce, soy sauce, and vinegar. Visit them at blisgourmet.com.

Cangshan Cutlery

Cangshan combines the best qualities of Western and Eastern style designs, materials, and workmanship to create unique knives for all levels of culinary creatives and professionals. Their passion is to build and craft distinctive, practical, and stunning knives that will last for years to come. Visit them at www.cangshancutlery.com.

Chef Works

Chef Works is the leading manufacturer and distributor of chef clothing and uniforms for restaurants and hotels worldwide. For the avid home cook, the active griller, or dinner party enthusiast, there's no other resource. Outstanding service and selection for every need. Chef Works has outfitted all their restaurants from top to bottom and they experience firsthand the level of quality and craftsmanship. Visit them at www.chefworks.com.

KitchenAid

Outstanding quality for cookware, cutlery, small and major appliances. They are the absolute complete resource for every piece of high-end cooking equipment and appliance. I use KitchenAid brand in my home, and recommend it to anyone I meet. Superior quality, outstanding service, and a century of innovation and manufacturing in the United States. Visit them at www.kitchenaid.com.

KitchenAid Commercial

The toughest and highest-performance equipment available in the commercial market today. Power your passion with KitchenAid Commercial. This new line of KA products will reinvent many of the kitchen industry staples. Newly designed and superior products will revolutionize your kitchen operations and efficiency. Visit them at www.kitchenaidcommercial.com.

Lumbertown Woodworks

Chris Sowa is a culinary instructor, industry professional, and extremely talented woodworker creating masterful cutting boards from the direct perspective only a chef could provide. Visit Chris's Etsy store for a full listing of his creations, or online at www.lumbertownwoodworks.etsy.com.

Melissa's Produce

A full-service operation that supplies culinary professionals as well as home cooks with staples, exotics, and Melissa's full line of organic produce. When recipes dictate specific ingredients and local sourcing presents a challenge, Melissa's is *the* choice for high-end products shipped directly to your doorstep. Visit them at www.melissas.com.

Tendon

Canvas and leather goods made in Michigan. Todd Hancock has been sewing and handcrafting the highest quality canvas and leather goods since 2009. For unmatched craftsmanship custom work, visit www.etsy.com/shop/tenden.

Terra Spice Company

Premium spices, spice blends, dried chilies, extracts, dried fruits, and vegetables. The highest quality products available in the market today. We utilize Terra Spice Company for all our salt, spice, dried herb, and specialty thickening agents. Visit them at www.terraspice.com.

Tilit

Tilit is the source for retail chef wear and custom uniforms. They are a family-run business manufacturing entirely American-made products. Thoughtfully constructed kitchenware and aprons appropriate for any level of cooking facility. This is kitchen-inspired modern garments with a casual, yet crisp approach. Visit them at www.tilitnyc.com.

ABOUT THE AUTHORS

Executive Chef & Coauthor Matthew Pietsch

Matthew is the executive chef and co-owner of the celebrated restaurant Salt of the Earth located in Fennville, Michigan, as well as Principle Food & Drink in downtown Kalamazoo, Michigan. Chef Matthew's food focus begins with sourcing the highest-quality ingredients and then processing these ingredients as simply as possible to honor the ingredients' integrity, as well as the individuals who worked so tirelessly to produce them.

A West Michigan native, Chef Matthew has been in the culinary and hospitality industry since 1997. As a college graduate of the culinary arts, Chef Matthew was inspired by an apprenticeship with the US National Pastry Team in 2004 and worked throughout West Michigan for several years as executive pastry chef. Later, he relocated to Detroit, where he operated the famed Opus One kitchen, which is where he began working extensively with seafood, taking great pride in the sustainable seafood movement while educating patrons and the public on what it means to eat sustainably, particularly when it comes to bycatch. Teaming up with Iron Chef Michael Symon to open Detroit's upscale steakhouse Roast set the stage for Matthew to relocate to Fennville in 2009, where he launched his first restaurant, Salt of the Earth, and in 2015, introduced Principle Food & Drink to downtown Kalamazoo.

Today, Chef Matthew serves up fresh, sustainable seafood, and is passionately devoted to preparing and serving various bycatch whenever possible. Chef Matthew commits his passion and energy to furthering the experiences of his guests through the provision of genuine and thoughtful hospitality while supporting the local community and movement of responsible sourcing, ingredient quality, and environmental sustainability.

Coauthor James O. Fraioli

James is a talented and experienced cookbook author, and a 2014 James Beard Award Winner for *Culinary Birds.* He has twenty-six cookbooks to his credit, with additional books currently in production.

Seasoned, skilled, and recognized for both the speed and grace of his writing, Fraioli's cookbooks have been featured on The Food Network and *The Ellen DeGeneres Show.* The author is notorious for teaming up with talented up-and-coming chefs as well as acclaimed celebrity chefs and world-renowned restaurants to showcase the best the culinary world has to offer. Fraioli's cookbooks have appeared on dozens of national radio shows, including *Martha Stewart Living Radio.* The author's beautiful and well-crafted books, continually noted for their exceptional prose, high production value, exquisite photography, and savory subject matter, have received further praise from such esteemed publications as *Forbes, Reader's Digest, Oprah Magazine* and the *New York Times.* His other popular seafood cookbooks include the award-winning titles *Ocean Friendly Cuisine* and *Wild Alaskan Seafood.* Visit him online at www.culinarybookcreations.com

INDEX

CONVERSION CHARTS

METRIC AND IMPERIAL CONVERSIONS

(These conversions are rounded for convenience)

Ingredient	Cups/Tablespoons/Teaspoons	Ounces	Grams/Milliliters
Butter	1 cup = 16 tablespoons = 2 sticks	8 ounces	230 grams
Cheese, shredded	1 cup	4 ounces	110 grams
Cream cheese	1 tablespoon	0.5 ounce	14.5 grams
Cornstarch	1 tablespoon	0.3 ounce	8 grams
Flour, all-purpose	1 cup/1 tablespoon	4.5 ounces/0.3 ounce	125 grams/8 grams
Flour, whole wheat	1 cup	4 ounces	120 grams
Fruit, dried	1 cup	4 ounces	120 grams
Fruits or veggies, chopped	1 cup	5 to 7 ounces	145 to 200 grams
Fruits or veggies, puréed	1 cup	8.5 ounces	245 grams
Honey, maple syrup, or corn syrup	1 tablespoon	.75 ounce	20 grams
Liquids: cream, milk, water, or juice	1 cup	8 fluid ounces	240 milliliters
Oats	1 cup	5.5 ounces	150 grams
Salt	1 teaspoon	0.2 ounce	6 grams
Spices: cinnamon, cloves, ginger, or nutmeg (ground)	1 teaspoon	0.2 ounce	5 milliliters
Sugar, brown, firmly packed	1 cup	7 ounces	200 grams
Sugar, white	1 cup/1 tablespoon	7 ounces/0.5 ounce	200 grams/12.5 grams
Vanilla extract	1 teaspoon	0.2 ounce	4 grams

OVEN TEMPERATURES

Fahrenheit	Celsius	Gas Mark
225°	110°	¼
250°	120°	½
275°	140°	1
300°	150°	2
325°	160°	3
350°	180°	4
375°	190°	5
400°	200°	6
425°	220°	7
450°	230°	8